Make It Yourself

Illustrations by
Ruth Hartshorn

CHILTON BOOK COMPANY
Radnor, Pennsylvania

Make It Yourself

a consumer's guide to cutting household costs

Dolores Riccio & Joan Bingham

ACKNOWLEDGMENTS

Thanks to our editor, Glen Ruh,
for his help and encouragement, and to
Pat Westphal for her finishing touches.

Design by Adrianne Onderdonk Dudden
Manufactured in the United States of America

Library of Congress Cataloging in Publication Data
Riccio, Dolores, ———
  Make it yourself.

  Includes index.
  1. Home economics—Handbooks, manuals,
etc. 2. Recipes. I. Bingham, Joan, joint
author. II. Title.
TX158.R5 1978 640 77-14689
ISBN 0-8019-6672-8
ISBN 0-8019-6673-6 pbk.

1 2 3 4 5 6 7 8 9 0   7 6 5 4 3 2 1 0 9 8

To my husband, Rick, who helped in everything
from testing to typing,
and to my daughter, Lucy-Marie

D.R.

To my daughters, Sally and Stephanie—
and to Peter

J.B.

Contents

2 Foods

3 Cosmetics

4 Home Remedies

Want to Join a Small Rebellion?

We've started our own revolution against the cult of consumerism. Instead of buying every new home product that slides off the assembly line, we're choosing fewer items that have greater versatility. With a minimum number of basic supplies, we find we can create most of the things we need or want around the house.

This homemaking from scratch has many benefits. The money saved is of prime importance. While the cost of everything is skyrocketing, most incomes are limping far behind. By making things ourselves, we save money and take added pleasure in not being ripped off by manufacturers who combine a few cheap substances into one high-priced product. Why should we pay them to mix ingredients that we can very well mix ourselves?

In addition, we're healthier because we don't ingest as many unnecessary preservatives, inhale dangerous aerosol propellants, or otherwise fall victim to the overabundance of chemicals found in many commercial products.

There's also the satisfaction of learning how things are put together—the materials, the methods, the expertise involved. And we take pride in the feeling of self-sufficiency that comes from being able to provide for our needs without running to a store every day.

And then there's the sheer fun of it—because making things *is* fun!

Our purpose in writing this book is to share with you the formulas and shortcuts we have discovered, so that you, too, can enjoy the satisfaction and savings to be found in making it yourself. You will be familiar with most ingredients we use. If you are in doubt about where to get any specific item, the Sources of Supplies will give you that information. Everything we use is readily available.

The time required to make most of the products in this book is less than you would imagine. It's just a matter of trading a little time to save a lot of money.

We're especially interested in economical, effective alternatives to prepackaged home care items, convenience foods, cosmetics, and health care products. Each trip to the supermarket brings the consumer face to face with a myriad of household cleaners. All are proclaimed as work-savers, and each seems to have a different purpose—the idea is that you should buy them all. Your furniture will shine, your windows glisten, your pots and pans gleam, and you'll be able to see yourself in the dishes. Your laundry will be the envy of all your neighbors, your sheets will be soft, and your socks won't stick together in the dryer. No marauding fly or ant will dare to cross your threshold. Your home will have a fragrance reminiscent of lemon, spring flowers, or pine, instead of stale cigars and fried fish. If you avail yourself of all these wonders (plus others too numerous to mention) your pocketbook will be considerably lighter. In the chapters that follow, we suggest many inexpensive, easy, and safe homemade alternatives.

The battle of the food market has turned into a full-scale war. While prices escalate, the desirability of food products declines with every preservative, emulsifier, artificial color, imitation flavor, and chemical enhancer added. Today most package labels read like pages from a chemistry book. Those tiny jars of baby food, too, can add up to a king-size expense without increasing the healthfulness of baby's meals. Even the family pet has not escaped unscathed. Fido can't tell you that the appetizing picture appearing on the can bears little or no relation to the palatability of its contents, but you can see for yourself how much more your pet enjoys homemade food and biscuits, and you'll enjoy the dollar savings. In this book, we've provided recipes for better, cheaper, and more nutritious ways to feed your families while kicking the convenience-food habit.

The products offered by our country's leading cosmetic manufacturers are made with simple ingredients readily available to all of us at a fraction of the cost charged for name brands. But all the creams and conditioners in the world won't make you a beauty if you don't start with well-nourished skin and hair. We offer easy formulas for natural homemade cosmetics instead. We don't guarantee that they'll solve all your beauty problems overnight, but they will save you a great deal of money, and they will improve and maintain the health of skin and hair. We have also included in our cosmetic section bath preparations that we find beneficial and delightful.

Americans spend millions of unnecessary dollars yearly on over-the-counter drugs. Yet many medically endorsed home remedies for burns, itches, and sleepless nights are common substances found in any home. A knowledge of what to reach for in case of small accidents and illnesses can often prevent them from turning into something more serious. In this book, we review the effective home remedies that can be used for first aid and also provide a list of necessary medical supplies (and those on which you don't need to waste your money). We give recipes, too, for soothing medicines our grandmothers used to make.

We've also included some of the household crafts of yesteryear that we find challenging today. Making soap, candles, and cheese, for example, are all art forms in themselves, to be enjoyed for the pleasure of making them and the pride you can take in each finished product.

But these are only samples of the many necessities and luxuries that can be made from scratch, often from materials you would ordinarily throw away, and always from easily obtainable substances. We don't believe in waste or unnecessary expense, and our book is dedicated to avoiding them. *Make It Yourself* is our small rebellion against consumer rip-offs. We hope you'll join us!

1
Household
Products

Making Your Own "Miracle" Cleaners

A hidden cost in your grocery bill is the number of household cleaners you pile into your cart at the supermarket. The encouragement for many of these purchases comes from TV commercials in which just picking up a can of some new product brings a muscular man in through the window to do the job for you. Or he may arrive at night, like the good brownies, to scrub unseen while you sleep. We all know that real life, alas, is not a bit like these commercial vignettes, that we will wake up to find kitchen grease undisturbed by the purchase of a miracle cleaner.

Meanwhile, a lot of money is wasted on household products. You can save yourself 50 percent or more of this expense by making many of these products yourself, using some of the same materials that manufacturers use in theirs. And you don't have to be a chemist to prepare these home recipes. Chances are you already have a number of useful cleaning agents around the house, and any ingredients you may need to buy are both inexpensive and readily available.

A few low-cost cleaners have been around since Grandma's day and suffer

R.H.

only from a bad press that claims they can't possibly work as well as the newest chemical formula (which may contain the same active ingredient). You pay dearly if you believe this myth.

Excellent cleaners, both old and new, can be mixed at home for far less than you pay for the commercial equivalent—mixing at the factory always costs you more. You may even pay for the trouble of lugging home water, if water is part of the formula, when you could very well turn on the faucet at home to dilute the cleaning agent to its proper strength.

The recipes and suggestions that follow were chosen because the materials are common substances that cost little, the mixtures are easy to make and to use, and the results are satisfying. Try them and enjoy the savings!

One word of warning, however: NEVER mix ammonia and chlorine bleach because that particular combination creates a deadly gas. Both ammonia and chlorine bleach are perfectly safe when used alone or mixed with many other more harmonious substances, including plain soap.

T.L.C. for Furniture

Furniture polishes are either oil or wax based. Oil gives a mellow lustre and an antique look. Wax provides a glossier finish and a more wear-resistant surface. Choose either an oil or a wax finish for each piece of furniture. In other words, don't put an oil polish over wax or wax over oil.

Linseed Oil Polish

1/2 cup denatured alcohol
1 1/2 cups water
1/2 cup raw linseed oil

Mix alcohol with water in a jar. Add linseed oil. Cover tightly and shake vigorously. Apply to clean wood surfaces, using a soft cloth and a moderate amount of the oil polish. Wipe off excess and buff to desired gloss. Always shake before using. *Note:* Oily rags are a fire hazard and should be discarded when you're through using them.

Lemon Oil Polish

This was a favorite many years ago and is recently in vogue again.

1 pint mineral oil (which is the same thing as paraffin oil)
2 teaspoons oil of lemon

Mix together. Rub on with a soft cloth and buff.

Grandma's Furniture Polish

1 tablespoon turpentine
2 tablespoons white vinegar
1/4 cup olive oil

Used faithfully with a very soft cloth, it gives furniture the mellow lustre of fine antiques. *Note:* Turpentine is flammable.

Spray Polish

Any of the preceding oil polishes can be put into a spray bottle. Use just as you would that expensive stuff in the aerosol can!

Paraffin Oil Polish

$^1/_2$ cup white vinegar
$^1/_2$ cup denatured alcohol

$^1/_2$ cup paraffin oil (mineral oil)
$2^1/_2$ tablespoons rottenstone powder

Blend the first three ingredients together. Then stir in the rottenstone powder. A piece of old toweling makes a good applicator. Rub until the article shines.

R.H.

Beeswax Polish

1 cup beeswax
$^1/_2$ cup turpentine
oil-based wood stain (optional)

Flake beeswax and melt it, either by putting it into a jar and standing the jar in a basin of hot water, or by putting it in the top of a double boiler over simmering water. Remove from heat and cool slightly. Stir in turpentine. Add the turpentine away from any heat source because it is flammable. If you would like this polish to have a particular color, such as maple or mahogany, you can use oil-based stains in small amounts to tint it. On oak furniture, however, it's really better to use a transparent polish lest the oak be darkened too much.

Apply the polish with a pad of cheesecloth. Let it dry for a few minutes, then buff with a soft cloth.

Carnauba Wax Polish

Carnauba wax is a product of the Brazilian wax palm tree. It yields a harder wax surface than beeswax and lasts longer, but it requires more elbow grease to buff it.

¹/₂ cup carnauba wax	¹/₂ cup turpentine
¹/₂ cup paraffin wax	oil pigment (optional)

Flake carnauba and paraffin waxes and melt them, either by putting them in a jar and standing the jar in a basin of hot water, or by putting them in the top of a double boiler over simmering water. Remove from heat and cool slightly. Stir in turpentine. Keep mixture away from any heat source, since turpentine is flammable. This polish may be tinted with oil pigment, as in the preceding recipe for Beeswax Polish.

Apply polish with a pad of cheesecloth. Let dry a few minutes, then buff with a soft cloth.

Wicker Cleaner

1 teaspoon Soft Soap (see page 43) or liquid detergent
1 tablespoon borax
2 quarts warm water

Mix all ingredients in a bucket or large basin. Wash the article without getting the wicker too wet. Rinse, and let the wicker dry near an open window.

Wax Remover

When too much wax builds up on furniture, it may be cleaned off with a cloth moistened in turpentine. If the build-up is excessive, you can use 0000 steel wool instead of a cloth, but test this method on the furniture finish first, in an inconspicuous place. *Note:* Turpentine is flammable.

Bric-a-Brac Duster

Dust intricately carved pieces with an old shaving brush dipped *very* lightly into a liquid polish (just enough so that the brush will pick up dust).

White Rings

If you can get to the ring before it penetrates, buff it with toothpaste on a soft cloth to remove the mark.

If this doesn't work, cover the ring with petroleum jelly and leave it there overnight. Then rub off the jelly and buff.

If the ring is too deep to be helped by petroleum jelly, make a paste of rottenstone powder and linseed oil. Rub it in with the grain of the wood until the ring disappears.

As a last resort, you can remove the wax finish and re-wax with fresh polish.

Grease Marks

2 tablespoons white vinegar
2 cups warm water

Mix together and use it to wash off the grease marks. Then immediately dry with a soft cloth. Wax and buff the surface.

Heat Marks

Mix cigarette ashes and linseed oil. Spread over the mark and leave the treatment there until the next day. Then rub it off, wax, and buff.

Ink Stains

Make a paste of lemon juice and salt to bleach out ink stains on light-colored wood.

Wood Bleach

To remove the color stain finish from an article made of wood, choose a hot, sunny place. Then swab the finish with full strength chlorine bleach and keep wetting it with the bleach until the wood is as light as you want. Protect everything you don't want bleached from getting spotted or streaked while you work.

Scratches and Cigarette Burns

If a burn occurs on wood, carefully scrape out the burned part. Try not to damage the surrounding surface while doing this. With a cotton swab, apply a bit of stain to match the rest of the article. If the mark is not very deep, a thick coat of paste wax should fill it. For a very minor scratch, you can even use a fresh nut meat of a matching hue to restain the wood to its original color. Wax and buff.

Keyboard Cleaner

Ivory piano keys that have yellowed may be cleaned with a mild bleach such as lemon juice. Mix it with whiting (powdered chalk) and apply it to the keys. Let it dry; then brush it off. Don't let the dust fall between the keys. Wash and buff dry.

Plastic piano keys can be cleaned with just a damp cloth.

Paints and Stains:
Coloring Your World

Believe it or not, there are paints you can make at home that will rival any store-bought paints, and the one below for Milk Paint will far surpass any of them for durability. Excellent stains can be made at home, too. They are a fine choice for use on woods that have a lovely grain you'd like to show off.

Milk Paint

The early American colonists made their milk paint from the milk used to boil berries. The result was an attractive gray color, which may be why so many of the beautiful New England homes of that era were gray.

This paint will not wear off, *ever!* It's great stuff if you're using a color you'll want to live with for a long time. Stripping it is a long arduous process that's done by first applying ammonia, allowing it to dry thoroughly for about four days and then applying bleach to the article. Do the stripping outdoors or in a well-ventilated room.

Milk paint, like so many other things, has been modernized. Here's an updated variation on the old theme.

1 1/2 cups dehydrated milk powder or crystals
1/2 cup water
water-based color

Mix milk and water until it's the consistency of paint. Blend in enough color to make the desired hue. If the paint is too thick, add more water. If it seems too thin, add more milk powder.

Brush on as you would any other paint, but let the first coat dry at least 24 hours before adding a second coat. Let this dry for another three days before using the article. This finish will take a great deal of abuse.

Dark Stain

1/4 cup alcohol   1 quart water
1/4 cup powdered logwood extract   1/8 teaspoon potassium chromate

Dissolve the powdered logwood extract in alcohol. Dissolve the potassium chromate in water. Combine the two mixtures and let stand for half an hour. Rub into sanded wood surface.

Yellow Stain

2 tablespoons powdered turmeric
1 cup alcohol

Mix ingredients thoroughly. Strain through cheesecloth and apply with a soft cloth or paint brush. For a deeper yellow, add more turmeric.

Tough Coat

Try this for a varnished surface that will withstand heat.

1 cup linseed oil
1/2 cup turpentine

Mix together and paint on an unfinished wooden surface. *Note:* Turpentine is flammable. Oily rags should be discarded when you're through using them.

Whitewash

This is as good for painting cellar walls as it is for whitewashing fences.

1 pound salt
1 gallon water
5 pounds hydrated lime

Dissolve salt in heated water. Add hydrated lime and stir to the consistency of a medium-thick paste. Brush on surface with large paint brush.

Paint Remover

When the painting job is done, if you find that some of the paint is on your hands, try removing it with trisodium phosphate and water.

Banana Oil Paint Remover

To remove unwanted paint or varnish from wood, try this formula.

$^1/_2$ cup acetone
$^1/_2$ cup benzene
$^1/_2$ cup banana oil or amyl acetate

Mix all ingredients together and apply with a cloth to painted surface. Rub in and let stand for 5 minutes before rubbing off with a rag or paint scraper.

Note: This mixture is flammable and strong smelling. Use it in a well-ventilated room away from any flame.

Kitchen Quickies

No-Rust Scrubbers

Fill a short, wide-mouthed jar $^1/_3$ full of Soft Soap (see page 43). Store plain steel wool in the jar, covered, until needed to scrub pans. The steel wool can be used again and again, because immersion in the soap keeps it from rusting. If you want smaller scrubbers, just cut a pad of steel wool in half with scissors (it will help sharpen the blades of the scissors, too).

Scouring Powder

1 part powdered pumice
1 part powdered soap

Mix together and store in a shaker.

Pinch Hitter for Steel Wool

Use crushed egg shells for scrubbing pots when you run out of steel wool.

Drain Cleaner

Pour $^1/_3$ cup coarse salt into the drain. Follow with 1 quart boiling water. Used twice a week, this treatment should keep your kitchen sink free of clogs.

Clog Cleaner

For a sluggish drain, pour $^1/_2$ cup baking soda into it, followed by 1 cup white vinegar. Wait a few minutes, then rinse with very hot water.

Enamel Cleaner

How do you get an enamel pot or pan clean when you're not supposed to scrub it? Fill the pan with water, and add 2 tablespoons baking soda for every quart of water. Soaking will sometimes do the job, but boiling is faster. If additional scrubbing is needed, use salt instead of an abrasive scouring powder.

Glass Coffee Pot Cleaner

It sometimes happens that one leaves an automatic coffee maker on the burner too long, and the coffee is reduced to a bilious brown syrup that stains the pot. In that case, let the glass container cool, then rinse it. Fill with warm water and 2 teaspoons baking soda. Let it soak for a half hour. Rinse again. Repeat the application, if necessary.

For regular cleaning, rub with a damp sponge dipped in baking soda to remove coffee stains. Rinse well.

Metal Coffee Pot Cleaner

A stained percolator can be cleaned by filling it with water to which you've added:

1 teaspoon borax
1 teaspoon detergent powder

Bring the water to a boil and allow the mixture to work for a few minutes. Rinse. Wash thoroughly, then rinse again.

Tannin Cleaner

To remove the stains that accumulate inside teapots or mugs, dip a damp sponge in baking soda, rub, and rinse clean. This cleaner will remove tannin without scratching surfaces.

Kitchen Disinfectant

Salt is a quick nontoxic disinfectant for kitchen use. If you want to clean out a sink or a dishpan in which to rinse food, pour salt on a wet sponge and use it as you would scouring powder.

General Kitchen Cleanser

For countertops, appliances, and almost everything in the kitchen except aluminum and wood, a solution of $1/4$ cup ammonia in 1 quart warm water does a fast, thorough job.

Heavy-Duty Kitchen Cleanser

$1/2$ cup TSP (trisodium phosphate)
2 gallons hot water.

Mix together. Wash soiled areas with it, then rinse with warm water. This is great for greasy walls, enamel-painted woodwork, and floors.

Thermos Bottle Sweetener

A sour thermos can be prevented if it is washed promptly after each use and stored with the cap and stopper *off*. However, there's always the time you forget the thermos in the car for three days. In that case, wash, rinse, add 1 teaspoon baking soda, and fill with hot water. Let the thermos soak for an hour or two. Rinse thoroughly.

If the thermos has become stained from carrying tea or coffee, use a bottle brush with a mixture of 1 tablespoon white vinegar and 1 cup warm water to clean it. If you don't have a bottle brush, put crushed egg shells into the thermos with the vinegar mixture. Close the cover, and shake it, Baby! Rinse well.

Oven Muscle

The fumes from straight ammonia will loosen baked-on oven grease for easier cleaning. Pour 1 cup or more ammonia into an old glass or enamel dish and set it in the oven. Shut the oven door and leave it for a few hours, preferably when you're not going to be in the kitchen if you don't like the smell of ammonia. (We leave it there overnight.) Later, remove the dish, and clean with an old sponge. Use steel wool on the stubborn places. (You'll find this inexpensive treatment works as well as any of the special preparations on the market.)

Rack and Grill Cleanser

Ammonia is tops for cleaning oven racks and outdoor grills. Soak the racks or grills in a solution of $1/2$ cup ammonia per gallon of water. After a half hour, the burned-on grease will be loosened for easy cleaning, but wear rubber gloves for this job.

Refrigerator Cleaner

Use $1/4$ cup baking soda in 1 quart warm water to wash the inside of the refrigerator. On the outside, use $1/4$ cup ammonia in 1 quart warm water. Rinse, and dry with a piece of old toweling.

Getting Around Buttons and Dials

Cotton swabs kept in the kitchen are handy for cleaning between buttons and around dials. Just dampen them in your regular cleaning solution, but be certain the appliance is unplugged when you clean. Don't use an ammonia solution on aluminum.

Salad Wash

When washing leafy greens, especially if they've come directly from the garden, put $1/4$ cup salt into the first rinse water. It will make all the little creatures that may be nested inside the leaves float out to where they can easily be flushed away with the next rinse.

Salad Bowl Finish

If you've bought an unfinished salad bowl, the only nontoxic finish you can use is plain mineral oil. Time and salad dressings will make the bowl a rich, beautiful color some day!

Bread Board Lightener

You can lighten an old bread board by rubbing it with the inside of a squeezed lemon half (something to think about the next time you make lemonade!).

Hand Cleaner

Fruit and vegetable stains can be cleaned off hands with a lemon wedge. If you've handled anything with a strong odor, such as garlic or sardines, try white vinegar or tomato juice to deodorize your hands.

Grease on hands can be cleaned with shampoo straight from the container. It leaves the sink clean, too!

Metal Magic

Silver Polish

Mix ammonia with whiting (ground chalk sold at hardware stores) to form a paste. Polish silver, rinse well, and buff dry.

Hand rubbing gives silver its lovely lustre. Don't use "dip it" polishes—they're super quick but they destroy the subtleties of the finish. Don't use a salt polish, because salt pits silver.

Tarnish is oxidation, and polishing rubs it off. Salad dressings, eggs, and fruit juices are the chief culprits when it comes to causing tarnish. Exposure to air causes tarnish, too, but it takes longer. Protect silverware from oxidation when it's not in everyday use by wrapping it in plastic wrap.

Silver Polishing Cloth

1 cup warm water
1 tablespoon ammonia
1 teaspoon whiting

Mix the ingredients together in a basin. Soak an old thin cloth napkin or tea towel in this mixture. Hang it up to dry over the basin. Use it to give a quick once-over to silver articles as needed.

Emergency Silver Polish

Ordinary toothpaste will shine up silver when you're out of polish (or upstairs and you don't want to go down). As with any polish, thorough rinsing is important.

Copper Polish

Mix equal parts of salt and flour. Add enough white vinegar to make a paste. Polish the article with this paste, rinse well, and dry completely with a towel to avoid streaking.

Or, for a fast treatment, as soon as a copper-bottomed pan comes out of the dishpan (while it is still wet), sprinkle with salt, using about the same amount you would if it were scouring powder, pour vinegar on a wet sponge, and polish; then rinse and dry. What occurs is a chemical reaction that requires no scrubbing to restore discolored copper to its former glory.

Brass Polish

Apply salt and vinegar or lemon juice with 0000 steel wool to uncoated brass or bronze. Rinse, dry, and buff. Worcestershire Sauce will also polish brass. It sounds wacky, but it works!

Pewter Polish

1 tablespoon turpentine
1 tablespoon linseed oil
  rottenstone powder

Mix turpentine and linseed oil. Add enough rottenstone powder to make a paste. Polish the pewter with this paste and wash in warm, soapy water. Rinse well, and buff dry. *Note:* Turpentine is flammable.

Lacquered or Coated Metal

Never wash lacquered metal in hot water! This cracks the finish, and then there's nothing you can do to make it look right again except to take all the lacquer off and start over—a ghastly job! If you have lacquered candlesticks and wax drips on them, chill the candlesticks to remove as much of the wax as possible in one piece. Then use *warm* water only to remove the rest of the wax. To give coated metal a lustre, polish with a few drops of olive oil on a soft cloth.

Aluminum

Boiling eggs, steaming foods, and even boiling plain water will discolor aluminum. In fact, there's very little good that can be said for this metal in the kitchen, but, if you have aluminum pans, you can prevent some staining by adding a tablespoon of vinegar to the pot when you boil eggs or steam puddings.

When stains can't be prevented, fill the pan with water and add 2 teaspoons cream of tartar to every quart of water; boil to brighten. Finish by polishing with steel wool and TSP (trisodium phosphate); rinse clean.

Chrome

Chrome is easy—it never requires any special treatment. Shine it with a soft dry cloth, or, if it's really dull, dip a damp sponge in baking soda and buff it with that. Rinse and dry.

Stainless Steel

In areas where the water is hard, stainless steel sinks and utensils tend to look spotty. A water softener, such as borax, applied with a sponge will solve this problem.

Gilt Frames

Clean gilt picture and mirror frames with turpentine on a soft cloth. *Note:* Turpentine is flammable.

Cast Iron

To season a new cast iron pan, grease it with any vegetable oil and put it in a warm oven for 2 hours. Do this after every wash for a few weeks. Then consider the pan seasoned and care for it by washing with soap and water, followed by really careful drying.

If you don't use the pan regularly or you don't dry it carefully enough, it may develop a rust spot. Scrub it well with steel wool and re-season the pan as you did when it was new.

Rust Preventative

This is good to use when storing a metal object you fear may rust.

$^1/_2$ cup melted lard
1 tablespoon rosin

Mix the ingredients together. Be sure the surface of the article is dry and rust-free. Rub the mixture on with a soft cloth, making sure not to miss any places.

Making Jewelry Sparkle

An Ounce of Prevention

Remove your rings before immersing your hands in hot water. Delicate gems can be damaged and fake ones glued into their settings can be loosened by hot water. Among those precious and semiprecious stones that can't take the dishpan are aquamarines, rubies, opals, pearls, sapphires, and emeralds. (You *don't* wear your emeralds while washing up, do you?)

Jewelry Brush

A very soft old toothbrush makes a good jewelry cleaner for getting into intricate links and carvings.

Delicate Gems

The stones mentioned above that should not be immersed in hot water can be cleaned with warm soapy water, with the exception of pearls. Rinse, dry, and buff.

Pearls

Glycerin on a soft cloth can be used to shine pearls. Real pearls, say the experts, benefit by being worn as much as possible, even to bed. They absorb the body's oils and become softly lustrous.

Diamonds

Like many hard precious stones, diamonds can be given a quick sparkle by polishing with a dab of cologne on a soft cloth. A dental assistant we know recommends cleaning engagement and wedding rings by immersing them in an effervescent denture cleaner for a minute or two.

Because they are hardy gems, diamonds can also be cleaned with whiting made into a paste with water, should they need a real polishing. Rinse and dry.

Gold Chain

A dull gold chain can be brightened by dipping it in a solution of 1 part ammonia to 3 parts soapy water. Rinse and dry.

Gold and Silver

Both gold and silver can be cleaned with toothpaste on a soft old toothbrush. As with any cleaning agent, it must be washed off thoroughly. Dry the article and buff to the desired gloss.

Copper

Clean copper jewelry with salt and vinegar (or lemon juice) made into a paste. Rinse, dry, and buff.

Platinum

Clean platinum with warm water into which you have put a little liquid detergent. Rinse, dry, and buff.

Lacquered Metals

Never expose lacquered metals to hot water because this will crack the finish. Use a bit of olive oil on a soft cloth to clean them.

Cameos

Dip an old soft toothbrush into warm soapy water to clean a cameo. Rinse and dry with an absorbent cloth.

Brightening Up the Bathroom

More unnecessary cleaning preparations are manufactured and sold for the bathroom than for any other room in the house, with the possible exception of the kitchen! Since you are only dealing with two or three kinds of soil, it stands to reason that a few simple cleaners are all that are needed: a disinfectant, something to remove soap film, and something to dispose of mildew and an occasional rust spot.

Tile Cleaner

Tile gets splattered and dulled with soap film, but it shines naturally when dulling soap film is removed. Here's a fast way to remove the film.

1/2 cup white vinegar		2 tablespoons TSP (trisodium phos-
2 quarts warm water	OR	phate)
		2 quarts warm water

Wash tile with either solution, and then rinse thoroughly. Wipe dry with an old towel for that polished look.

Grout Cleaner

Dip an old toothbrush into straight white vinegar and go over the blackened grout. You won't even have to scrub. Rinse well. If you're working in the shower and the shower head is detachable, use that for the rinsing.

Toilet Bowl Disinfectant

Pour 1 cup chlorine bleach into the bowl and use the brush to go over all surfaces. (Don't splash the seat!) Let set for 15 minutes. Use the brush again, then flush. Clean the outer surfaces with soap and water.

Ring-Around-the-Tub

To quickly remove that grimy ring, pour white vinegar on a damp sponge and rub clean. Or use a tablespoon of water softener. Using 1 teaspoon of liquid detergent in every tub of water prevents these rings, if you can get your family to remember to use it.

Bathtub Brightener

This works wonders on a rusty or discolored bathtub.

cream of tartar
hydrogen peroxide

Make a paste of these ingredients. Apply them to the tub and scrub with a nail brush. Rinse clean.

Bathroom Floor Cleaners

For a tile or linoleum floor, use one of the same cleaners you used on the wall tile (above) or the recipe on page 20.

Ceramic Soap Dish and Toothbrush Holder

Pour straight alcohol or white vinegar into the soap dish. Proceed with other cleaning and come back to it in 10 minutes. Use a piece of old toweling to absorb the alcohol or vinegar. Gummy soap residue will come with it.

Use alcohol to clean and disinfect the toothbrush holder. A cotton swab is good for getting right into those toothbrush holes.

Plastic Soap Dish, Shower Curtain, and Shower Caddy

Mildew and soap film are often the culprits causing soiled plastic bathroom accessories. Put them all into the tub with water to cover, to which 1½ cups chlorine bleach has been added (stir the water and bleach well). Let the items soak until clean. Rinse and drain. The chlorine bleach will have cleaned the tub as well, so just give it a few swishes with a sponge.

Brushes and Combs

Put brushes and combs into the bathroom sink with warm water and ½ cup ammonia. After 20 minutes, rinse and let them dry on the bathroom windowsill.

Naturally Nice Deodorizers

Tannin and Lemon

Mix the juice of 1 lemon with 1 quart of strong tea. Strain through a paper coffee filter. Store in empty spray bottles (old cologne bottles are pretty) and keep wherever needed. (Spray the air, not the walls!)

White Vinegar

Fried fish, boiled cabbage, and stale tobacco odors can be exorcised with a bowl of vinegar. This deodorizer can be hidden in an opaque vase for living room use.

Tomato Juice

Plain tomato juice or a mixture of equal parts tomato juice and white vinegar are time-honored remedies for skunk spray, should your dog be indiscreet enough to chase a wood kitty. The same remedy works on odors that cling to a cook's hands, like garlic, onion, or sardine oil.

Vanilla

If the odor of fresh paint is distasteful to you, mix ½ tablespoon vanilla into each quart of paint. It will not change the color.

Charcoal

A form of carbon that absorbs odors, charcoal kept in any closed space, such as a closet, will keep the place sweet-smelling. Charcoal briquettes work well for this. Keep them out of the reach of children and pets.

Cloves

Whole cloves, not the ground variety, will sweeten your clothes closet. Tie the cloves into small cheesecloth bags, or, if you don't mind taking a bit more trouble, make Pomander Balls (see page 128).

R.H.

Dry Mustard

Mix 1 teaspoon dry mustard with 1 quart water to deodorize bottles. Rinse well.

Baking Soda

Well-known for its usefulness in refrigerators and kitty litter pans, baking soda is an all-purpose deodorizer. Try sprinkling it in the bottom of the dishwasher if you don't run it very often, especially in the summer.

Burnt Match

Sulphur is a deodorizer, so for a quick cure, strike a match to dispel an offending odor.

Orange Peel

This is the most aesthetically pleasing house deodorant. Roast orange peel over a very low heat for a delicious aroma throughout your rooms.

Fast Work on Walls, Floors, and Woodwork

Wall Cleaners

We are of the school of thought that it's better to start washing walls at the top and work down, providing you do so with a dampened (not dripping) sponge and that you wash the sponge out frequently.

2 teaspoons ammonia
1 cup borax
1 gallon warm water.

Mix together in a bucket. After washing the walls, rinse them and wipe dry.

Here is another good wall cleaner.

¹/₄ cup TSP (trisodium phosphate)
1 gallon warm water

Separate rinsing is not necessary.

Enamel Paint Wash

1 tablespoon sal soda (washing soda, a cheap strong cleaner)
1 teaspoon Soft Soap (see page 43) or liquid detergent
1 quart warm water

Mix together. Wash, then rinse with clear water. Fantastic!

Flat Paint Wash

This cleaner is only mildly abrasive and will not harm the paint.

1 cup Soft Soap (see page 43)
1 teaspoon ammonia
1 tablespoon whiting

Mix together. For spots and stains, dip a small piece of old toweling into the mixture. Rub the spot. Rinse well with plain water.

For all-over cleaning, combine ¹/₂ cup of the mix with 1 quart of warm water. Dampen a cloth in this. Wash, and rinse well.

Wallpaper Treatment

A really thick washable wallpaper can be lightly sponged with plain water. A thinner paper, no matter how it was advertised, is better not washed. However, there are two common substances that will absorb the dirt without injuring the paper. One is art gum. The second is stale bread (yes, bread!) with the crusts cut off, rubbed gently over the surface of the wall. Some sources swear that rye bread is the most efficient, but either white or rye works.

A paste of fuller's earth and dry cleaning fluid will remove grease stains from wallpaper. Apply paste, let dry, and brush off.

Varnished Wood Cleaner

¹/₂ cup white vinegar
2 quarts warm water

Mix together. Dampen a soft cloth with it to wash the wood. Wipe dry with another cloth.

Wood Floor Cleaner and Polish

Never use water on a wood floor. Instead, clean with a liquid polish (see pages 4–6) in a small area at a time. Use a wax-based polish on a floor that has been previously waxed, an oil-based polish on a floor finished with oil: Do this even if ultimately you intend to finish with a paste wax, because paste will not clean as well. Use 0000 steel wool dipped in turpentine to remove stubborn grease and dirt. After the polish has dried thoroughly, buff to the desired gloss.

Wax Removers

Turpentine will remove the wax from a wood floor. On linoleum or tile, use the following recipe:

> 1 cup ammonia
> 1 gallon warm water

Mix together. Swab floor freely with this mixture. Wipe up a few minutes later with lots and lots of clean rags. Do not let this mixture dry on the floor covering. One way to prevent this from happening is to clean one small (4 feet by 4 feet) area at a time.

Linoleum or Tile Floor Cleaner

> $^1/_2$ cup TSP (trisodium phosphate)
> 1 gallon warm water

Mix together. Wash the floor with a mop dipped in this mixture and wrung out. Rinse with a mop dampened in plain water. (Do not use a dripping wet mop for either operation.)

All Around the House

Glass Cleaners

A 28-ounce bottle of plain (not sudsy) ammonia will make 28 quarts of window cleaner, and a better bargain you can't find anywhere!

> 2 tablespoons ammonia
> 1 quart water

Mix together and pour into an empty spray bottle for convenience in using. Wash the glass and wipe it dry with half sheets of newspaper for a no-cost, no-lint finish. Some element in printer's ink gives a special polish to glass. Use not only on windows but any glass that needs cleaning—glassed pictures, glass doors, mirrors, glass tops for tables, TV screen (make sure the set has been turned off for awhile), ashtrays, etc.

Either white vinegar or alcohol can be substituted for ammonia, if you wish, using the same proportions.

Fill another spray bottle with the mixture, close it in a plastic bag, and put it in your car, along with half sheets of newspaper. You'll be grateful to yourself some muddy day!

Upholstery Cleaners

First test an unseen portion of the fabric to see if the material will take water. If so, mix up the following:

> $^1/_4$ cup pure soap flakes
> 2 tablespoons borax
> 1 pint boiling water

Allow this mixture to cool. Then whip to make a frothy lather. Use only the lather, and keep the whole operation as dry as possible. Work in a small area with a brush dipped in the lather. Rinse with a cloth dipped in clean water and wrung as tightly as possible.

For grease spots, make a paste of baking soda and water. Rub on the spots and let dry. Then remove with a soft brush or vacuum cleaner.

Chocolate can be removed by rubbing pepsin powder into the stain. Leave it on for a half hour; then sponge off with a damp, not wet, cloth.

For the treatment of other spots and stains on fabric, see the next section, "Removing Spots and Stains."

Carpet Cleaners

A gray area on a carpet can be treated with an absorbent powder such as cornstarch. Sprinkle the carpet with cornstarch early in the day; vacuum up several hours later. Or make a paste of fuller's earth and water. Apply it to the gray area, allow it to dry, and then loosen with a brush. Finish by vacuuming.

Cornmeal can also be used as an absorbent cleaner on carpets or thick-pile upholstery. It is used the same way as cornstarch.

When something is spilled on a carpet, wipe it up immediately. Avoid rubbing—use a blotting action instead.

Food stains and general-purpose cleaning can be taken care of with the following recipe:

2 teaspoons white vinegar
2 teaspoons liquid dish detergent
2 quarts warm (not hot) water

Mix together. Before washing, first test a small section of carpet to make certain it is colorfast. Then wash very lightly, a small area at a time. Do not rub hard and do not soak the carpet. Blot up excess moisture.

Animal urine stains can be treated as follows:

1/4 cup white vinegar
1 cup warm water

Stir together. This mixture will neutralize the urine and deodorize the spot, which is not only necessary aesthetically but also helps prevent the pet from coming back to do the same thing in the same place. If the rug is a fine Oriental (heaven forbid!), the best thing to do is to immediately flush the urine-stained area with plain water. To do this, raise the rug and place a basin under the area to be cleaned. Force the water *through* the fibers of the soiled spot without letting it run over the rest of the rug. When the area has been thoroughly flushed, blot up the excess moisture, and keep the rug raised for quicker drying.

To remove other kinds of stains, see the next section, "Removing Spots and Stains."

Fireplace Brighteners

Brick and stone are both very absorbent, so don't use any kind of soap solution to clean them. Rinse as you may, some trace of the soap will remain in the form of a white deposit. Instead, use a brush and clear water.

A burned place can be rubbed with straight white vinegar.

For red brick, another brick is used to restore the bright color to dark places. Just rub one brick (freshly broken is best) against the other. For stone, a bit of powdered pumice can be used on a particularly stubborn spot.

Slate is cleaned and polished with linseed oil. Be sure to wipe up the excess. To lighten marble, use white vinegar or lemon juice. Swab on full strength, rinse and let dry.

On andirons, use 0000 steel wool. (For a brass polish, see page 13.)

Log Lighter

Nature has a natural assist to kindling. In the fall, collect pine cones. They look attractive in a basket, and they are laden with pitch to make them an ideal fire starter, much more efficient and long lasting than newspaper, safer than any chemical preparation.

Leather Cleaners

To remove grease from leathers other than suede, beat up an egg white to a good frothy consistency. Dip a soft cloth into the froth, and rub until the grease is gone.

On suede, use only a soft brush to clean. If the suede is really soiled, you can make a paste of fuller's earth and water. Apply, let dry, and brush clean.

For general cleaning of all leathers except suede, use this solution:

1/4 cup Soft Soap (see page 43)
1 pint warm water

Mix together. Dip a cloth into the solution, but wring it out so the cloth is damp, not wet. Wash the leather. Rinse with another damp cloth.

Leather Conditioners

This conditioner is great for stiff, dry leather:

1 part lanolin
1 part neat's-foot oil

Warm the lanolin until it melts, then mix it with the neat's-foot oil. Apply with a soft cloth and let set for a few minutes. Blot up excess. The next day, if the leather still seems dry, repeat the process.

To condition dry leather shoes, you can use straight castor oil. Apply, let set, and remove excess with a soft cloth. White leather can be conditioned with petroleum jelly.

Leather Waterproofer

1 tablespoon tallow (rendered animal fat; for how to make it, see page 39)
2 tablespoons lanolin
1/4 cup neat's-foot oil

Warm the tallow and lanolin together until they melt. Mix with the neat's-foot oil. Rub into the leather with a soft cloth.

Oil Paintings

If the oil painting is an original Rembrandt, or something similar, you will, of course, allow an expert to do the job. Less exalted oil paintings (not watercolors, not prints) can be cleaned with a peeled, sliced potato and linseed oil. First, go over the surface of the painting with a fresh slice of potato. Then, gently sponge with a damp cloth. Finally, polish by wiping with a soft cloth dipped into linseed oil.

Books

The best way to dust books is with the brush attachment (be sure it's clean) on a vacuum cleaner. The second best way is to use a large clean paint brush kept especially for that purpose.

Leather book bindings can be conditioned with the following:

1/4 cup lanolin
1/3 cup neat's-foot oil

Warm the lanolin. When it has liquified, add the neat's-foot oil. Apply to the binding with a gauze pad. Be very careful not to touch any other part of the book. Stand the book up, fanned out, to dry.

Flowerpots

When clay flowerpots get encrusted with a white deposit, which is caused by fertilizer salts working through the clay, they can be cleaned by immersion in the following bath:

1 cup white vinegar
1 gallon hot water

If the flowerpots are too big to be entirely covered by the mixture, turn them once during the process. Leave overnight. The next day, run them through the dishwasher, or wash with hot soapy water and rinse very well.

Marble

If possible, let the marble heat in the sun before cleaning. Then use chlorine bleach full strength over the entire surface. Rinse with plenty of clean water and let dry. If necessary, repeat the application in an hour. (Be sure you protect surroundings from bleach splatters!)

Outdoor Plastic Furniture and Plastic Tablecloths

The closer you live to the city, the grimier these get!

1 cup ammonia
1 teaspoon liquid detergent
1 gallon warm water

You'll need more than one sponge for this job, as well as some clear water for rinsing. Mix ingredients together. Wash the items and rinse them well. *Note:* Don't use this mixture on anything made of aluminum.

Mildew Killers

Mildew can suddenly become widespread, especially during damp, hot weather. You may discover the fungi in all sorts of likely and unlikely places, like fine old books and the insides of leather shoes. Keep in mind that this growth has several serious enemies: sun, any kind of dry heat, chlorine bleach, alcohol, and plain old soap and water. Which remedy you select depends upon how delicate the article to be treated is. First, to make certain it *is* mildew, put just a drop of chlorine bleach on the fungi. If it fades, it's mildew.

Mildewed painted wood can be treated with this chlorine solution:

2 cups chlorine bleach
6 cups water

Mix together. Test first to be sure the paint won't discolor. Weaken the solution, if necessary. Wash the mildewed paint surface with the solution and then rinse.

Mildewed leather should be treated with the following solution:

1 cup rubbing alcohol
2 cups water

Mix together. Test the leather in an inconspicuous place first. Don't soak the article; apply the solution with a damp, not wet, sponge. Rinse with a damp cloth. Finish with a leather conditioner (see page 22). If the alcohol mixture cannot be used according to your test, try the conditioner alone.

Mildewed books need to be dried out, either by putting them in the sun or by turning on an electric heater in the room. Wipe the bindings lightly with a mixture of:

1 cup white vinegar
2 quarts warm water

A *mildewed concrete floor* can be treated with:

1 pint chlorine bleach
2 gallons water

Just wash with this mixture, rinse, and then open all the windows so that a thorough drying out can take place.

Putty

Need a little putty to fill a crack before painting or to seal a window pane? No need to rush out to the hardware store, if you have these in the house:

whiting
linseed oil

Put a little whiting in a saucer. Add enough linseed oil to make a paste. Use as you would any putty.

Removing Spots and Stains, and Brightening Up Blue Monday

Every family has one! The member who makes keeping clothes clean a real challenge. It may be Junior who spills chocolate milk on his new white shirt, or the tomboy with grass stains and mud on her outfit from sliding into homeplate, or even Dad may be the culprit, wiping his greasy hands on his clothes when he's finished fixing the car. Each stain calls for individual treatment, but cheer up! It's not so difficult.

The first thing to remember about stains is that generally they should be treated as soon as possible. There are a few exceptions to this rule, as you'll see when you read this section, but almost every substance becomes more difficult to remove the longer it sets. The second thing to remember is that if you try to remove a spot with the wrong substance, you may make the stain permanent.

Before you tackle any stain, read the fabric care label attached to the garment. Even homemade clothes should have this label (fabric shops are required to include a care label with every piece of material sold). Most (but not all) washable fabrics can also be dry cleaned. If not, they bear a label reading "Do not dry clean." Fabrics that are labeled "Dry clean" may not be washed.

Right after a spot occurs, carefully blot up the excess liquid so that it won't be absorbed into the fabric. To do this, lightly touch the liquid with a paper towel or a piece of cotton. Don't press down! The absorbent material works like a wick, drawing up the liquid. Keep turning the paper or cotton and touching a clean part of it to the liquid until all of the excess has been absorbed.

Next, if you're dealing with a light, nongreasy spill and if the fabric is washable, use a little cool water to dilute the stain. First place several layers of paper toweling under the stained area. Put just a few drops of water on the spot. Quickly blot this up with clean paper toweling or cotton. Add a few more drops of water and blot again. Continue to do this until the absorbent material stays clean. This may be all that is required to remove the spot. If so, wash the garment as you normally would.

If the stain on a washable or nonwashable fabric is light but of a greasy origin, it should be cautiously sponged with dry cleaning solution.

Warning: Dry cleaning solutions are flammable and poisonous! Use them carefully. Always work in a well-ventilated space far away from any flames or sparks. Don't allow the solution to come in contact with your skin. Work with rubber gloves. Never use dry cleaning fluid in a washing machine. Always keep the solvent in an unbreakable, tightly covered, labeled container stored in a cool place out of the reach of little hands. It sounds scary, but dry cleaning fluid is safe as long as you treat it with respect.

Before you treat a stain with anything, test the fabric to be sure that the solution won't damage it or cause more staining. Do your testing on a hem, a seam, on the inside of a pocket or anywhere else on the garment that won't show if the test turns out badly. If your test spot shows signs of shrinking or stretching, or if the color fades or runs, seek professional help for removing the stain.

Because some of the cleaning solutions you'll be working with are quite strong, it's important to choose a work surface that won't be damaged by them. A good choice is a glass pie plate, placed upside down on a kitchen counter that is protected with an old sheet or a piece of foil.

Sponging, flushing, and tamping are three important techniques used in spot removal. A brief description of each follows.

Sponging. When instructions say to sponge, place several layers of paper toweling or a layer of cotton on top of an inverted glass pie plate. Put area to be cleaned on top of the paper or cotton, with the stained side down (the side of the fabric from which the stain entered the material). With a piece of cotton dampened (not soaked) in the cleaning solution, clean the affected area. Start in the middle of the stain and work out. Don't enlarge the stain by cleaning out any further than necessary, and don't stop in a definite circle. Feather the outer edges as you clean. This is less apt to leave a ring on the fabric.

If the stain is a heavy one or doesn't come out right away, change the absorbent material under the fabric whenever it shows signs of picking up the stain. And use a new, clean piece of cotton whenever this shows stain.

Use just enough cleaning solution to remove the stain, and use a light touch in applying the solution. The object is to remove the stain, not to rub it in. When

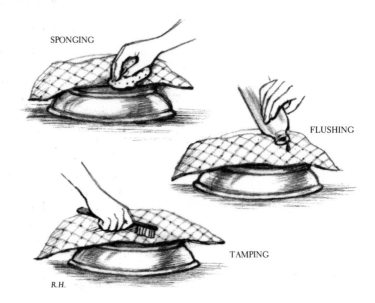

SPONGING

FLUSHING

TAMPING

R.H.

you have sponged away as much of the soil as possible, place the wet area between several layers of paper toweling and blot up the excess liquid. If a stain is stubborn, sponge it with a little more cleaning solution, letting it soak into the fabric for an hour or more and adding solution whenever necessary to keep spot damp.

Flushing. This technique is generally used after a stain remover has been applied. Many of the solutions which remove stains also cause new ones if they're left in the fabric. Flushing prevents this. To flush fabric, place several layers of paper toweling or other absorbent material on top of an inverted glass pie plate. Place stained material, stain side down, on top of this. Apply the flushing solution (often water) to the stained area with an eye dropper, very slowly, waiting for the material under the stain to absorb what's been applied before adding a few more drops. When the toweling is saturated, replace it with clean, dry toweling—otherwise, the unabsorbed liquid will go back into the material you're trying to clean.

If you're flushing with water, you can hold the stained part of the garment under a slowly running faucet or fill a bowl with water and dunk the stain in and out of it. Change water frequently if you use this method.

Tamping. A small brush is used for tamping—a toothbrush or a new round shoe polish brush will do. When tamping, place the soiled area of the garment directly on an inverted glass pie plate. Use the brush as you would a hammer: come down repeatedly—but gently—on the stain. Be sure that you hit the material with the ends of the bristles and not the side of the brush. Don't bang the fabric. When using this method you must watch carefully to avoid fabric damage. Loosely knit fabric is more easily hurt than a closely woven, stronger material.

Following are some common stains and methods for removing them.

Alcoholic Beverages

Blot up any spill that hasn't been absorbed by the fabric. Then sponge with a solution of:

    1 gallon warm water
    1 teaspoon liquid detergent
    1 tablespoon white vinegar

After sponging, soak the garment overnight in the solution. If the spot is still visible in the morning, test the garment for colorfastness with chlorine bleach. Then mix:

    1 teaspoon chlorine bleach
    1 tablespoon water

Sponge the spot and, after a few minutes, flush with water to remove any traces of bleach.

Blood

Blood stains that have set can be extremely stubborn. So, as soon as possible after staining has occurred, flush the area with cold running water until stain has almost disappeared. Then sponge with detergent and warm water. Flush again with cool water. If garment is washable, wash as usual. If not, let the stained area dry. For a stain that is old, try sponging with ammonia or hydrogen peroxide, then flushing with water.

Butter

With a dull knife, scrape off any butter that hasn't been absorbed into the fabric. Dust the stain with cornmeal, or, if the fabric is dark, use fuller's earth. Let stand for 5 minutes, then brush off. If grease hasn't been absorbed, reapply fresh cornmeal or fuller's earth and leave it on for another 5 minutes. Launder as usual if the fabric is washable. If it isn't washable, sponge the spot with dry cleaning fluid.

Chocolate

Liquid stains—the kind that come from chocolate milk—should be blotted up quickly to prevent the spot from spreading. Then they should be sponged with warm water. When the garment is dry, if there is still a trace of the spot, remove it by tamping with a solution of water and liquid detergent. Let this set for a few minutes and then flush out with clear, warm water. If the garment is washable, launder as usual.

A chocolate stain that is made by a candy bar or other thick chocolate should be treated as follows. First scrape off any chocolate on the top of the fabric. Sponge the spot with a solution of:

    1 tablespoon borax
    1 cup warm water

Flush with water. If further treatment is needed, make a paste with borax and water and work it into the stain. Allow this to remain on the material for an hour or so. Flush well with warm water, and, if fabric is washable, launder as usual.

Chlorine

If your bathing suit has chlorine stains, try this:

    1/4 teaspoon color remover
    1/2 cup cool water

Mix ingredients together and sponge the solution into the stain. Flush the spot with cool water.

Coffee

The difficulty involved in removing a coffee stain depends largely on two things: whether the stain is fresh and whether the coffee was black or had cream in it.

    Black coffee stains attended to immediately aren't very troublesome. Sponge the stain with a solution of:

    1 teaspoon detergent
    1 teaspoon white vinegar
    1 cup water

Rinse well. If the material is washable and strong, pouring boiling water through the stain should flush it out.

    Cream adds to the problem by creating a greasy stain. Sponge the spot with dry cleaning solvent, allow it to dry, and, if fabric is washable, wash as usual.

    This remover is also a good one for coffee stains:

    1 egg yolk
    1 tablespoon dry cleaning solvent

Mix ingredients well and sponge into the stain. Allow it to set for 5 minutes, and then flush with tepid water. If the water is too warm, it will cook the egg and you'll have created a new problem.

Cosmetics

Brush off any surface stain. Then sponge the area with a solution of:

    1 cup warm water
    1 teaspoon ammonia
    1/2 teaspoon detergent

If the stain is stubborn and the material is sturdy, try tamping with this same solution. If the material is washable, soak it in the solution for about 20 minutes. Then flush it with warm water and launder.

Cream Sauce

If the fabric is washable, flush the stain with warm water. Then launder in detergent and warm water. If it is not washable, sponge the spot with dry cleaning solvent, allow it to dry, then flush with cool water.

Dyes

These are tough stains to deal with even when they're fresh and, when they've been allowed to set, they're practically impossible to get out. If the material is washable, try sponging the affected area with a solution of:

1 quart cool water
1/2 teaspoon detergent
1 teaspoon bleach

Flush the stain with cool water, and soak it overnight in cool water and detergent. If the stain is still visible in the morning, tamp the area with a brush dipped in undiluted detergent. Flush well with cool water.

For fabric requiring dry cleaning, tamp the stain with cool water and then sponge with detergent. Flush out the detergent with cool water. Blot the fabric dry between layers of paper toweling.

Egg

If the egg has hardened, scrape off as much as you can with a dull knife. Try sponging the area with tepid water. If the spot still remains, make a paste of:

1 teaspoon pepsin powder
a few drops of water

Work this paste into the spot and allow it to remain for about an hour. Flush the spot with cool water. *Note:* Before using pepsin powder, be sure to test printed fabrics for colorfastness. Pepsin destroys certain dyes while it is fine with others.

A stain from the white of an egg usually responds to this treatment: dissolve 1 teaspoon salt in 1 cup water, and sponge the solution into the stained area. Then flush it out with cool water.

Egg yolk should be tamped with the suds from a solution of detergent and cool water, then flushed with cool water. If the spot remains, sponge with dry cleaning solvent, and, if fabric is washable, launder as usual.

Fingernail Polish

This stain often responds to light sponging with chemically pure amyl acetate, a flammable substance that must be used with extreme care. (Test fabric before using amyl acetate.) If the fabric is washable, flush well with cool water after sponging, and launder it immediately. If the garment is not washable, blot off excess amyl acetate between layers of paper toweling and allow the spot to dry thoroughly.

Fruit

Always flush fruit stains with cool water as soon as possible. Some of these stains, such as those from lemon and other citrus fruits, seem to disappear when they dry. Don't be fooled, though—they will reappear, and when they do will be very stubborn. So use the cool water treatment even if you don't think it's necessary.

Many other fruits leave an ugly purplish-blue mark. This mark often releases after a sponging with lemon juice followed by flushing with boiling water. Never use soap and water on a fruit stain. It sets it!

Glue

Some glues such as epoxy cement simply won't come off. But most plastic glues, if they have not hardened, will respond to being sponged with warm water and detergent. If the glue has set, try soaking the spot in boiling hot white vinegar for about 20 minutes and then flushing it with plain boiling water. If the fabric is washable, launder immediately.

Grass

These stubborn stains often require many steps before they disappear. First, sponge the stained area with dry cleaning solvent, blot the excess between two layers of paper toweling, and let the fabric dry. If the stain still remains, sponge it with chemically pure amyl acetate (test fabric before using). Follow this by flushing with dry cleaning solvent. Let the fabric dry again. If the spot still persists, flush with cool water and tamp with white vinegar. Flush with water and allow to dry again before sponging the spot with alcohol. Flush with water a final time. By now the grass stain should be gone.

Gravy

Sponge the spot thoroughly with cool water. Follow this by sponging with detergent suds and flushing again with cool water.

If the stain isn't gone and the garment is washable, soak it in a solution of:

1 quart cool water
1 tablespoon ammonia
1 teaspoon salt

Rinse spot well and launder garment as usual.

If the fabric is not washable, sponge the spot with dry cleaning solvent.

Grease

On fabrics that require dry cleaning, apply a paste made of fuller's earth and dry cleaning solvent. Work the paste into the spot, let it dry, and then brush it off.

Another method is to place an absorbent material (cotton, a sheet, or paper toweling) on an ironing board, place the garment stained side down on top of the absorbent material, and press it with as hot an iron as the garment will stand. Change the absorbent material often, until all the grease is dissolved.

Gum (Chewing Gum)

Chill gum and affected fabric with ice cubes. Then break the stiffened gum away from the fabric. If the gum isn't completely removed, try sponging it with dry cleaning solvent. Flush with warm water.

Ink

To remove black ink stains, make a solution of:

juice of 1 lemon
1 teaspoon of salt

Sponge or tamp this mixture into the soiled spot. Flush well with water and wash the garment immediately.

If this method doesn't work, try sponging the spot with chemically pure amyl acetate (test fabric first). Flush well with cool water after application. Turpentine sponged into an ink spot is also an effective remover. Follow this by thorough flushing with tepid water.

Iodine

If the stain is a new one and you get to it before it dries, try soaking the spot in milk for half an hour. Rub milk into the fabric with your finger. A fresh iodine stain can often be removed by soaking it in cool water and then working detergent into the spot, followed by flushing with cool water. If the fabric you're trying to clean isn't washable, try removing the iodine by sponging the spot with alcohol, then flushing with cool water.

Old iodine stains are more difficult to deal with, but they're by no means impossible. Try sponging soiled area with a solution of:

1 teaspoon sodium thiosulfate
1 cup warm water

Allow water to cool before applying the solution to the spot. Flush well with cool water.

Lipstick

If fresh, this stain can sometimes be removed by lightly blotting it with a piece of soft white bread. Any remaining lipstick should wash out after the area is sponged with detergent and water.

If the stain has set or if it doesn't respond to detergent and water, try working glycerin into it with your fingers or sponge glycerin into the spot. Flush well with cool water. If the garment is washable, launder as usual. A fabric that isn't washable can be flushed with ammonia followed immediately by water.

If the fabric is a strong one, you can try tamping it with straight white vinegar followed by a thorough flushing with warm water. Blot the fabric dry between two layers of paper toweling and let it dry. You may find that traces of the stain still remain. Sponge with alcohol and allow it to dry. If the stain still persists, try tamping with chlorine bleach followed by flushing with warm water. Be sure to test the fabric for colorfastness before using bleach.

As a last resort, dry cleaning solvent will usually remove lipstick stains from any fabric.

Mayonnaise

Mayonnaise contains egg, and the egg will cook right into the fabric if you use anything hot on it. If the fabric is washable, sponge the area well with cool water. If the fabric is a strong one, tamp it with cool water. This may take care of the problem, in which case you can launder the article as usual. If the stain is stubborn, wet it with cool water and sponge it with bicarbonate of soda. Leave this on for about 5 minutes, then flush the spot well with warm water.

On a nonwashable fabric stained with mayonnaise, you'll probably have to use a dry cleaning fluid.

Meat Juice

Follow instructions for removing blood stains.

Mildew

Mildew is a mold, and it should first be brushed off the fabric. Do this outside where the spores will not get onto other things.

For bleachable clothing, mix the following:

$^1/_2$ cup chlorine bleach
1 gallon warm water

Soak the clothing for a half hour. Then run through a regular washing cycle.

For unbleachable colored clothing (but not silk or wool) try this milder treatment:

$^1/_4$ cup lemon juice
1 teaspoon salt
2 quarts cool water

Proceed as for bleachable clothing.

If you get a nice hot dry day, you can spread articles of clothing outside on sheets to bleach in the sun.

Soaking a washable fabric in sour milk before laundering it will sometimes remove mildew stains.

If the stained material isn't washable, flush the stain (after brushing) with dry cleaning solvent, then sponge it with chemically pure amyl acetate (test fabric before using). Flush again with dry cleaning solvent and let the fabric dry thoroughly. If the stain persists, flush it with alcohol several times, letting the fabric dry between each flushing. Since mildew weakens fabric, it's not advisable to tamp.

Milk

If you get at milk spills right away, they usually can be rinsed off with clear, cool water. If milk is allowed to set or dry, it can leave a ring that's difficult to remove. Soft Soap (see page 43) or a paste made of soap flakes and water, worked into the spot with the fingers, often does the trick. Follow with a thorough flushing with warm water.

If the fabric is a nonwashable one, sponge the area with cool water. Then sponge the spot with dry cleaning solvent or chemically pure amyl acetate (test fabric before using).

Mud

Mud is one of those stains you don't touch until it's thoroughly dry. Then you should brush it off with a stiff brush. If the fabric is washable, sponge the spot with a mild solution of detergent and water, and launder as usual.

For a nonwashable fabric, after brushing off dried mud, sponge the stain with dry cleaning solvent.

Mustard

This can be a very difficult stain to remove from any fabric and it's impossible to remove it from plastic, such as a plastic tablecloth. If the fabric is not plastic and it's washable, sponge the stain while it's still fresh with warm water and detergent. Flush with warm water, and sponge again. Repeat this until there is no visible sign of stain. Then launder the garment as usual.

If sponging hasn't removed the mustard, soak the article overnight in very warm water and detergent before laundering. If the stain still hasn't come out, rub glycerin into it with your fingers, let it stand for 2 or 3 hours, then flush with warm water, and launder the garment.

On a nonwashable fabric, flush the spot with dry cleaning solvent, tamp, and then flush again with the solvent. Allow to dry. If the spot is still visible, sponge it with a solution of:

  1 tablespoon ammonia
  1 cup warm water

Flush with warm water. Repeat the ammonia and water treatment, if necessary, and flush again with warm water. If the stain still isn't gone, sponge it with a few drops of 3% hydrogen peroxide, let stand for 2 minutes, then flush well with warm water.

Pencil

Pencil marks on tightly woven fabrics can often be removed with a good, clean soft eraser. If the fabric is washable and the eraser fails to remove the mark, sponge it with detergent and water, flush with warm water, and launder as usual.

If the garment is not washable and an eraser doesn't do the job, flush the mark with dry cleaning solvent, then sponge with a mixture of 8 parts dry cleaning solvent to 1 part mineral oil. Dampen a piece of cotton with this solution and place it on top of the pencil mark, leaving it to soak for about 20 minutes. Then flush with dry cleaning solvent and allow the fabric to dry.

If the spot still remains, sponge it with warm water and reapply the cleaning solvent-mineral oil mixture. Follow this with a few drops of ammonia and tamp the stain. Flush again with water and allow the fabric to dry.

Perfume

When a delightful fragrance leaves an ugly stain, sponge it first with plain warm water. If this doesn't work, tamp the spot with a solution of 8 parts dry cleaning solvent to 1 part mineral oil. Let this stand a minute or two, then flush with water.

If the stain persists, cover it with an alcohol-soaked piece of cotton. This will draw the perfume out of the garment into the cotton. Change the cotton often so that the stain won't return to the garment. When the stain has all been absorbed, flush the spot well with warm water.

Perspiration

If the fabric is washable, make a solution of:

  2 tablespoons salt
  1 cup warm water

Rub the solution into the stain and let it soak for about 30 minutes before laundering. Or if you prefer, you may soak affected area in a solution of 3 tablespoons of white vinegar to every cup of warm water and then wash the garment. Colors that have faded from perspiration occasionally can be restored by sponging the area with ammonia and then flushing it with cool water.

If the fabric isn't washable, try holding the affected spot over a bottle of ammonia. The fumes may loosen the spots and they can then be sponged away with dry cleaning solvent.

Perspiration stains of the strong yellow type may need bleaching. Test the fabric first, then proceed by soaking the stain for about 5 minutes in a solution of 2 tablespoons of 3% hydrogen peroxide to every cup of warm water. Flush well with warm water.

Rust

Nonwashable fabrics with rust stains are best taken to the dry cleaner. But if the fabric is washable, there are several things you might try at home. Flush stain with warm water, then sponge it with freshly squeezed lemon juice. If the fabric is a strong one, flush it with boiling water. A fabric that's delicate can be held over a steaming pot instead, or flush lemon juice out of the fabric with warm water.

A combination of salt and lemon juice worked into the spot and allowed to dry before flushing it out with warm water often removes rust.

If these methods fail, try this:

1 part cream of tartar
1 part alum
enough water to make a paste

Mix the ingredients well to make a paste. Work this into the fabric and let it stand for 5 minutes before flushing out with warm water.

Salad Dressing

See Mayonnaise for creamy dressing and Grease for oil-based dressings.

Scorch

Those brown marks that come from a careless cigarette or an iron can be removed if the fabric hasn't been destroyed. Sponge with 3% hydrogen peroxide to which you have added a few drops of ammonia. Let this stand for about 5 minutes, but don't let it dry. Flush the spot with water and repeat the process if necessary.

A fabric that is thick and shows surface scorch but not fabric damage can be made to look right again by scraping off the scorched fibers with a nail file or a piece of sandpaper.

Shellac

Sponge the affected area with dry cleaning fluid. If the spot remains, apply a solution of 8 parts dry cleaning fluid to 1 part mineral oil and tamp the area. Flush with dry cleaning fluid and allow to dry. If the stain still shows, sponge it with alcohol. Then flush with water.

Shoe Polish

The method of removing shoe polish depends on the color of the polish. Black polish responds to sponging with turpentine followed by flushing with warm water and detergent, then flushing with warm water only. A washable garment should then be laundered.

Brown shoe polish should be sponged with alcohol and then flushed with warm water.

White shoe polish should first be treated by sponging the spot with a solution of 8 parts dry cleaning solvent to 1 part mineral oil. This should be followed by flushing with dry cleaning solvent. If this doesn't work, try sponging with chemically pure amyl acetate (test the fabric first), then flushing with the dry cleaning fluid. Allow this to dry thoroughly. If the spot remains when the fabric is dry, sponge it with water, then tamp it with white vinegar and flush with water. Repeat the process of tamping with vinegar and flushing with water three times. This should remove any but the most stubborn white shoe polish stain.

Tar

This is a messy stain which resists removal. First scrape off as much tar as possible with a dull knife. Then if the fabric is washable, place a lump of solid white shortening on top of the spot and leave it there for 3 hours. This will lift the tar so that, after washing, the garment should show no more signs of it.

Sponge nonwashable fabrics with turpentine. Change the absorbent material often. Use a light touch for sponging so that you won't push the tar into the fabric instead of removing it.

Vinegar

Stains caused by vinegar will generally disappear with the light application of ammonia and water at a ratio of 1 tablespoon ammonia to 4 tablespoons warm water. Flush with warm water.

Wax

With the awakened interest in candles, wax stains are turning up more frequently. Whether a fabric is washable or not, first scrape up as much wax as you can with a dull knife. Do this when the wax is thoroughly dry and brittle. If you attempt it when the wax is still soft, you're apt to work it into the fibers. When as much wax has been scraped off as possible, place the stained area between two layers of paper toweling or other highly absorbent material. Press with a warm iron. This releases the wax from the fabric, and it is taken up by the absorbent material. Change the toweling frequently until it no longer is absorbing wax.

If a spot of wax still remains, try sponging it with dry cleaning fluid. If the stain still persists, sponge it with a solution of 8 parts dry cleaning fluid and 1 part mineral oil. Flush this out with dry cleaning fluid. If the spot still remains, tamp with straight ammonia and flush with warm water.

Rub-a-Dub-Dub:
A Few Washday Tips

Presoaks

If a garment is especially dirty or has unidentifiable spots, you may be setting the dirt instead of cleaning it out when you put the clothing right into your washing machine without pretreating it. Clothes that look like they won't come clean in the regular wash can be put to soak in detergent and water for half an hour before washing. A tablespoon of ammonia added to the water will help loosen the dirt.

Ring-Around-the-Collar

This well-known washday pest usually responds to a treatment with warm detergent water before washing. Rub suds into collar and let it set for about 15 minutes before washing in the machine. If the collar is especially grimy, mix:

> 1 tablespoon ammonia
> $^1/_2$ teaspoon detergent
> 1 cup warm water

Work the solution into the collar and allow it to set for half an hour before laundering.

Laundry Sweeteners

For lovely smelling laundry reminiscent of fresh violets, add a piece of orrisroot to the final rinse water of your wash. Or if your clothes are to be ironed, add a few drops of your favorite cologne to the water you sprinkle on them.

Diaper Soak

If you have a baby in the house and wash diapers, soak them in a solution of:

> $^1/_2$ cup of baking soda
> 1 gallon of water

This keeps the house sweet smelling by solving the problem of diaper pail odor.

Colorfast Test

Most colored fabrics manufactured today are colorfast, but some can fool you. It's no fun to do a load of wash and find that everything comes out with a faint tinge from a garment that's bled. When you're washing something you're not sure of, it's best to test it first. Thoroughly dampen a portion of the hem or some other out of the way part of the garment. Place it between two pieces of blotting material (either cloth or paper toweling will do) and apply a warm to hot iron. If the color isn't fast, it will come off on the absorbent material.

Soaking a multi-colored article which isn't colorfast in saltwater before washing it by hand often keeps the colors from running into each other.

Anti-Static Aid

If you're out of those products that are supposed to eliminate the static electricity that makes your wash stick to itself, add a teaspoon of liquid detergent to the final rinse cycle in your washing machine.

Flame Retardants

More and more parents are concerned about flameproofing their children's clothing. Whether the commercial methods are safe and whether they wash out are debated issues. Here are two flameproofing solutions which are recommended by fire departments. Either one is effective, but they should be used after each washing or dry cleaning. If the article is washable, it should be soaked in the solution after the final rinsing, then dried. If the garment is not washable, it should be sprayed with the solution.

Note: These solutions are flame retardants. They *don't* make a fabric impervious to fire.

9 ounces borax
4 ounces boric acid
1 gallon water

Mix well and apply to garment.

Here's another fire-resistant solution.

1 part sodium-silicate
9 parts water

Mix well and apply to garment.

Wool Soak

This solution will clean washable woolens without scrubbing.

¼ cup borax
1 tablespoon laundry detergent (liquid is best)
2 quarts warm water

Mix together and stir to dissolve borax. Allow to cool. Put woolens in to soak for 20 minutes. Squeeze suds through gently, then rinse thoroughly in cool water. Do not wring, just press out as much water as you can and spread them out to dry on towels.

Starch

This makes a light starch, fine for clothing.

1 tablespoon cornstarch
1 pint cold water

Add water to the cornstarch, and stir to dissolve the cornstarch completely. Use as you would any starch, even in a spray bottle. It must be stirred each time before using.

Fabric Stiffener

Here's an easy way to stiffen light materials such as net or thin cottons.

1 tablespoon (1 package) unflavored gelatin
$1/2$ teaspoon borax
4 quarts water, divided

Measure 2 cups of the water into a small saucepan. Sprinkle the gelatin on the water, and dissolve over low heat, stirring constantly. Combine the gelatin mixture with the remaining water and borax. Dip the article to be stiffened, and hang it over a basin to drip dry.

Iron Cleaner

To clean the plate of an iron, you can use 0000 steel wool, whiting, or both. An occasional application of beeswax will make the iron glide over clothes much more smoothly. Coat a warm iron with wax, then iron off the excess on an old cloth.

Antifreeze for Laundry

If you must hang out clothes in winter, mix ½ cup salt into the last rinse, and they won't freeze.

Washing Machine Cleaner

Many washing machine repair bills are the result of soap build-up clogging the machine. To avoid this, once or twice a month run a wash and rinse cycle with water only and add 1 cup white vinegar to it.

The Art of Making Soap

Before soap became a giant industry (whose advertising campaigns spawned that great American institution, the soap opera), soapmaking was one of the vital household arts. All through the long winter, two household waste products were religiously saved for that important week in spring when they would be made into a year's supply of soap. It was almost a magical transformation, because these waste products were hardly synonymous with cleanliness—one was the accumulation of animal fats left from slaughtering and cooking meats, and the other was sooty ashes collected from stoves and fireplaces. These products provided the two main ingredients of soap—fat and lye. The combining process is called saponification.

The way soap works is this: the fat loosens the dirt with its slippery quality while the lye breaks down the resistance of stubborn soil. This allows the washing water to carry the dirt away. Due to its lye content, soap is an alkaline which neutralizes acids. The human body, as it happens, is slightly acid, so many stains on clothes are acid-based from the body's secretions. This makes soap ideal for washing skin and laundering clothes.

Wood ashes contain potassium carbonate (called potash, for short), and the first step in early soapmaking was to leach out this substance from the ashes. This was accomplished by alternating layers of ashes with hay and lime in a barrel. The barrel had holes drilled on the bottom, and it was fixed at a slant for slow but steady drainage. Clear water was poured into the top of the barrel, and a brownish liquid drained out the bottom. The lime reacted with the potassium carbonate, which is a mild alkali, to form calcium carbonate and caustic potash. The latter was the strong stuff wanted for soap making.

Meanwhile, the animal fats were rendered (melted) and strained. When rendered fat cools, it separates, and the top layer is called tallow. Tallow and caustic potash, combined when both are hot and stirred until thick, made the soap our greatgrandparents used. It was a soft soap, and remained so until a new type of lye, called caustic soda, was developed. Today, we can gauge the temperature precisely with thermometers, but, in the old days, a homemaker needed a lot of experience and a little luck to get it just right. In case she didn't feel adequate to the task, there were soapmakers who went from town to town offering their services and expertise at stirring and testing.

When the first commercially manufactured soap was sold in stores, it was cut from a large block in however many pounds the customer wanted, just like cheese. That was before Mr. Proctor and Mr. Gamble and the Pear's Company of England began to package their products in pre-wrapped, ready-cut bars.

Homemakers naturally hailed this as progress. It was a lot easier to buy soap in a neat little package than to spend a week in spring stirring a cauldron over an open fire.

Times change, however, and today the art of soapmaking is very much alive in our craft-oriented society. It is both challenging and satisfying to make home-made soap, which contains exactly the ingredients the maker prefers, perfumed or unperfumed as desired. It is really long-lasting, too, since it's denser than the commercial varieties. (Some manufactured soaps even have lots of air whipped in to make them float, so naturally these cakes disappear faster in water.) Homemade soap has more glycerin (it's in the tallow), which is soothing to the skin. It makes a unique gift, and it can be shaped in many attractive ways after the basic techniques have been mastered. And another thing about homemade soap—it's dirt cheap!

SOAP INGREDIENTS

Basic Soap

5¹/₂ pounds tallow
11¹/₂ ounces caustic soda (lye flakes)
4 cups water
¹/₂ ounce perfume oils, if desired

2 ounces optional ingredients: 2 ounces wheat germ oil OR 2 ounces cold cream OR 2 ounces oatmeal flour (ground in blender) OR 2 ounces cocoa butter

Castile Soap

4¹/₂ pounds tallow
2 cups olive oil
11¹/₂ ounces caustic soda (lye flakes)

4 cups water
¹/₂ ounce perfume oils, if desired

MAKING TALLOW

The first step in soapmaking is to render beef fat to make tallow. You can collect fat from trimming beef cuts—and just keep putting the trimmings into a plastic bag in the freezer until you have 12 pounds. But, if you're in a hurry to get started, you can also buy beef fat from whichever meat outlet will give you the best price. It's only a few cents a pound, so this will not call for much of an investment. Plain old beef fat is what you want, and you don't have to be fussy about it.

Render the fat in a large heavy kettle. Cover the bottom of the kettle with an inch of water and add a heaping tablespoon of salt. Cut up the fat and put it in the kettle. Cook over very low heat for 3 to 4 hours, or until most of the fat has been rendered. Some remaining lumps may be very stubborn, but those will be strained out. In the interests of kitchen safety, don't pick up that heavy kettle full of fat and pour it through the strainer. Instead, put the strainer (a fine meshed one) into a large pan next to the fat kettle. *Be sure the heat is turned off.* Dip out the fat and pour it through the strainer. A 2-cup Pyrex measuring cup will do the dipping job well, but towards the end you might want to use something smaller like a soup ladle. Discard whatever fat didn't melt.

Allow the rendered fat to cool to room temperature, then refrigerate it. When set, it will form three layers. The solid piece on top is tallow, which is all you will use from this. The rest is waste, and you can discard it. You will need 5½ pounds of tallow for your first batch of soap. It can be kept in the refrigerator (a week) or in the freezer until you are ready to use it.

WEIGHING THE INGREDIENTS

To weigh the tallow and other ingredients for soapmaking, you will need a food scale. Put an empty container, large enough to hold the tallow, on the scale. Write down its weight when empty. Then put the tallow in, and, when the scale registers the desired weight *plus* the weight of the container, you will have the right amount.

In weighing the lye, the same method is used. The lye you will be using, caustic soda, comes in dry flakes, but water will be added to it after weighing to make a solution.

Weigh carefully, because the success of your soapmaking depends upon accuracy.

MIXING THE LYE

Handling lye is tricky, and proper precautions must be taken to avoid burns. Dry lye (caustic soda) begins to burn when it contacts moisture, and you have plenty of moisture on your skin, so you don't want even one flake to settle on you through carelessness. Wear rubber gloves and a smock or copious apron when working with the lye, and protect all work surfaces. If a flake does settle on you, rinse it off with lots of cold water.

You'll need a 3-quart glass, enamel, or stainless steel container with a cover for the lye. After weighing the container, spoon in the desired weight of dry lye. Add the measured water into the container of dry lye. This will activate the lye and make it quite hot (about 200°F or 92°C.) Stir the mixture with a long-handled wooden spoon until all the lye is dissolved. Cover it and put the mixture in a safe place to cool off. This can be done the day before actually making the soap.

COOKING THE SOAP

Allow the whole afternoon when you are ready to make the soap. Cover all surfaces of your space with layers of newspaper.

First, prepare the molds for your soap. Any sturdy cardboard boxes will do. Keep in mind that you will want to cut the soap into bars as you decide on the size and shape of the boxes you want. (Gift boxes will probably be the most convenient. Shoeboxes may also be used. You will need two molds of shoebox volume.) Line the boxes with old pieces of sheet or pillowcase with sufficient excess to cover the top after the soap is poured. The lining of each box should be a single, smooth, well-fitted layer. Either poke the cloth carefully into the corners of the box, or cut the cloth at the corners to trim away some of the excess so it doesn't bunch up. Cut pieces of cardboard to use as covers on the boxes, if they don't already have covers.

Both the lye mixture and the tallow should be between 96° and 98°F (36°C) when you mix them, so have ready two meat thermometers with easy-to-read scales.

Now remelt the tallow in a heavy kettle. When melted, it will be too hot. Put it into a basin or dishpan of cold water to reduce temperature to 96° to 98°F (36°C). (If you are making Castile Soap, add the olive oil to the melted tallow at this time.)

The container of lye, now cool, can be heated by standing it in a basin of hot water.

When the lye and the tallow are both between 96° and 98°F (36°C), you are ready to add the lye to the tallow. Warm a large glass pitcher by putting hot water into it. Empty the glass pitcher. Carefully pour the lye solution into it. If it doesn't all fit, you can add the rest later. *Do not overfill it.*

Now pour the lye in a slow steady stream into the tallow while *stirring constantly.* (Avoid splashing while pouring the lye mixture into the melted tallow. If some splashes on your skin anyway, immediately rinse the area with lots and lots of cold water. Lye causes burns.) After all the lye has been added, keep on stirring until the mixture thickens. This could take more than an hour, so be prepared.

DRIBBLE DESIGN ON
TOP OF MIXTURE

R.H.

POURING LYE

The mixture is thick enough when it achieves the consistency of molasses. When you dribble some off the end of your spoon, it should not sink into the mixture but instead should leave a trail on the top. You should be able to dribble a design on top of the mixture. *It's important not to pour the soap into the molds before this stage is reached.*

Now is the time to add any of the special ingredients you wish to give your soap its unique character. A combination of perfume oils weighing a total of 1/2 ounce may be stirred in. Wheat germ oil, cold cream, oatmeal flour, or cocoa butter can be added, the total weight of these additions not to exceed 2 ounces. Blend well.

FILLING THE MOLDS

Put the lined molds next to the soap mixture on your work table. Dip the mixture out with a cup or ladle and pour it into the molds. Don't try to pour from the pan. When all the liquid soap has been poured, cover the molds with the remaining cloth, then with the cardboard covers, and put several old towels on top of these (this is to retain heat so the soap does not cool too quickly). Leave them there until the next day.

In 24 hours your soap should be hard enough to cut. If not, wait another day.

Remove the large cakes from their molds and peel off the cloth. Trim the soap by peeling off a thin layer all around, just as you would trim the rind off cheese. This will remove any caustic soda that may have worked its way to the surfaces of the cakes.

With a ruler and knife point, trace the lines that will form your bars of soap. Slice into bars with a sharp heavy knife. The bars may not be perfectly shaped, but they will have, as Willa Cather put it, "the irregular and intimate quality of things made entirely by human hand."

Let the soap air-dry at least three weeks before using. Then, lather up and enjoy!

TOOLS OF THE SOAPMAKER'S TRADE

Here is a review of the equipment needed to make soap:

*Food scale
Large, heavy kettle, stainless steel or enamel. It should hold at least 8 quarts
Large fine-meshed strainer
large pan in which to cool the rendered fat
wooden spoon, the longest one you can find
2-cup Pyrex measuring cup
soup ladle
rubber gloves
large apron or smock
3-quart container with cover (Pyrex, enamel, or stainless steel) to hold lye solution
2-quart glass pitcher
stack of newspapers
2 stainless steel meat thermometers with easy-to-read scales
2 basins (or 1 dishpan and 1 basin)
cardboard boxes for molds
pieces of old sheeting or pillowcases to line molds
extra cardboard for mold covers
several old towels
knife*

Note: Kitchen equipment used in making soap can be washed afterward and returned to its regular food-making duties.

THINGS THAT CAN GO WRONG

After the lye has been added to the melted fat, the mixture sometimes separates or curdles. If this happens, return the pan to the stove over low heat. Continue to stir. When the mixture is 130°F or 55°C (test with thermometer) remove from heat. Keep stirring until the desired thickness is reached.

If the soap does not harden, don't use it, because the distribution of lye will be uneven.

If the soap cake has bubbles that are filled with liquid, don't use it. The liquid may contain lye.

If you make any kind of mistake, don't be discouraged. Try again another day. Homemade soap is worth the effort, and, like any art, soap-making must be practiced to be perfect!

Soft Soap

Several recipes in this book call for Soft Soap, a jellied soap that dissolves easily in warm water. It has literally hundreds of uses around the house (in fact, it can be used for almost anything except in an automatic dishwasher), and it's made from what you would ordinarily throw away—the ends of soap bars (they don't have to be ends from homemade soap—any soap will do!).

Plain Soft Soap

2 ounces soap ends, shredded, *or* ¼ cup loosely packed pure soap flakes
1 cup water

Put the soap in a small saucepan with the water. Simmer, stirring, until the soap has melted. Strain through a tea strainer into a wide-mouthed jar. Cover. Soft Soap keeps indefinitely.

(Do save the soap ends—it's so much more economical!)

White Soft Soap

Make Plain Soft Soap, as above. Use only pure white facial-quality soap so that it may be used for cosmetic purposes (like shampoos).

Rose Face Wash

1 ounce shredded facial soap *or* 2 tablespoons white soap flakes
1 cup hot water
1 teaspoon alcohol
⅛ teaspoon oil of rose

Melt the soap in the hot water. Then stir in the alcohol and oil of rose.

Action Soft Soap

This is an all-purpose kitchen cleaner. After Plain Soft Soap has cooled slightly, add the following:

1 teaspoon ammonia
1 tablespoon powdered pumice

Soft Soap for Fine Washables

Add ¼ cup borax to Plain Soft Soap. Use with tepid water to launder fine fabrics.

The Art of Making Candles:
"Brighten the Corner..."

The romance of candlelight is back! And we think homemade candles glow just a bit brighter than commercial ones. We've discovered that candlemaking is more than putting a bit of string in a piece of wax—it's a true art form.

These are the things to remember for accident-free candlemaking:

1. *Before* you start to make a candle, have all the equipment at hand. This eliminates the temptation to leave the wax on the stove while you rush to get that forgotten something.

2. *Before* you start candlemaking, select a work area away from the stove and cover it generously with old newspapers.

3. *Before* you start candlemaking, place a box of baking soda and a large pan lid close to the stove. If a small fire should occur, sprinkle it well with baking soda and smother it with the lid. *Don't use water on it!* This will make the wax splatter and spread the flames quickly.

4. Never melt wax over direct heat. Not only is this a fire hazard, but it causes the wax to melt unevenly and scorch. Always melt wax in a double boiler or other sturdy container placed in a large pan of water.

5. Always allow ample room for expansion in the container you use for melting—wax expands when it's heated and contracts as it cools.

6. Always pour wax from a container with a spout, such as a coffee pot or a Pyrex measuring cup. This helps eliminate spilled wax. Hot wax burns. If you should spill any on yourself, don't try to pick it off. Plunge the affected area into cold water, just as you would any burn. When the wax hardens, you can peel it off.

7. Always pour wax at your newspaper-covered work area. Never pour it in the sink. If you spill on the newspapers, it won't matter. If you spill in the sink, the wax will harden in the drain pipe—a problem you don't need.

8. Melted wax gets hot! Handle pans and molds with pot holders.

9. Wear an apron, in case of spills or splashes. If you should get wax on your clothing, see page 35.

10. Candlemaking is not for children. Keep them out of the kitchen or work area until you're finished.

Most accidents occur when a veteran candlemaker gets careless and eliminates a precaution. The novice generally sticks to the rules and has no accidents.

CANDLEMAKING SUPPLIES

Wax

There are several kinds of wax from which to choose. Paraffin is a good wax for beginning candlemakers because it's inexpensive. This well-known wax comes in three types: (1) low-temperature paraffin, which melts at temperatures between 125° and 135°F (52° and 58°C); (2) medium-temperature paraffin, with a melting point of 140° to 150°F (60° to 65°C); and (3) high-temperature paraffin, which melts at temperatures between 160° and 170°F (71° and 77°C).

Another variety of wax, candle wax, is also available in the three types. It may burn a bit better, but it's also a bit more expensive.

Beeswax is unquestionably the finest wax for candles. However, it's not easy to work with because it tends to stick to the molds. Since it's also expensive compared to the other types of wax, we think it should be left for the veteran candlemakers. If you want to try it, we advise you to use 40 percent beeswax and 60 percent candle wax or paraffin. There's no doubt about it, beeswax burns beautifully!

The type of wax to use depends on the type of candle you wish to make. If you're using a metal mold, buy wax with a medium melting point. A container candle, which is burned in its mold (usually glass), does best if it's made from wax with a low melting point, while a hurricane candle, which is a thin wax shell that is placed over a votive candle, needs the added support given by wax with a high melting point. Use a wax with a low melting point when making candles in molds found around the house.

The melting temperatures of waxes vary greatly from manufacturer to manufacturer. If you're not entirely satisfied with the candle you've made, next time try wax made by a different company.

Candle wax and paraffin suitable for making candles are available in slabs weighing 10 or 11 pounds. Four good-sized candles can be made from one slab of wax.

You're bound to have wax left over from your candlemaking. Don't throw it away! Let it harden in a shallow pan, then break it into pieces and store them in a plastic bag. Next time you're making a candle of that color, you can add the saved wax to the melting pot.

Wicks

Some commercial molds tell you what wicking material and what thickness to use for best results with that mold. But if you're improvising and making molds out of things you have around the house, you must guess at it, but you will learn from experience. If you select a wick that's too small in diameter, it's liable to burn unevenly and keep going out. Use a thicker wick the next time you use a mold that size. On the other hand, if your wick is too large, it will smoke. Use a thinner wick next time.

To get an idea of the size wick you should use, browse in the candle shops and see what size wicking is used in molds similar in width to those you're going to use.

Wicking which is available in candle shops or hobby shops comes in two kinds: cloth wicking and wire wicking which is covered with braided cloth. The wire melts as the candle burns. Container candles, as well as any candles in which wicks are inserted after the wax has hardened, require wire wicks. Candles which are poured with the wick in and then unmolded before burning usually do well with cloth wicking.

Molds

There are so many things around the average home that make lovely molds for candles it's hard to choose one. Just remember that you have to be able to get the candle out once it's hardened (unless you're making a container candle). This doesn't mean that you can't use a mold which has a narrow opening, but if you do, you'll have to sacrifice the mold to get the candle out of it. A glass or china mold can be broken by wrapping it in a towel and breaking it gently with a hammer. Then you can add the wick if you haven't already done so. Milk cartons, margarine tubs, old Christmas tree ornaments, jelly jars, gelatin molds—in short, just about anything that will hold water—can be used as candle molds.

R.H.

Commercial molds produce fine candles. The metal ones give a particularly pretty sheen to the wax. Plaster molds are rather expensive and it's often difficult to unmold candles made in them.

Stearin

Stearin comes in powder or crystal form and is not an essential ingredient of candlemaking. It does, however, produce a firmer, brighter-burning, less brittle candle. The more stearin in the wax, the more opaque the candle. A candle that is about one-fourth stearin and three-fourths wax will be white. A general rule of thumb is that 3 to 4 tablespoons of stearin to every pound of wax equals a snow white candle. If the candle is to be a colored one, use only 1 tablespoon of stearin to every pound of wax. If you have a heavy hand with stearin, you'll end up with a soft, mushy candle.

There are times when stearin isn't desirable. You won't want to use it in hurricane candles because you want the wax to look as delicate and translucent as possible. Don't use stearin in wax that's to be used in glazing, since the purpose of glazing is to give the candle a shiny, see-through outer layer. If you're planning to glaze a candle with wax, set some aside for this purpose before you add stearin.

Some commercial waxes come with stearin already added. Be aware of this when you purchase wax.

Crystals

Another nonessential, crystals accomplish much the same thing as stearin, except they do not make the candle opaque. They are seldom used when stearin is an ingredient. You need only about 1 teaspoon of crystals added to a pound of wax to produce a hard candle with a shiny surface and superior burning beauty.

Dyes

Candle dyes come in three forms—powdered, solid, and liquid. We find that the powdered is difficult to work with. It's harder to mix and seems to get all over the place. Take a tip and leave it to the professionals.

Solid color, or color buds, are by far the simplest dyes to use. These are solid pieces of wax with a concentration of color. To use them, cut off a piece and melt it into the wax in the melting pot. If you have red, yellow, and blue buds, you can achieve most of the colors you'll want for your candlemaking by mixing them.

Liquid dye is measured with an eyedropper. If you opt to use it, you can make up your own dye buds ahead of time. Instead of using just a few drops in a large amount of wax to obtain the color candle you want, you can make wax buds with a little wax and a lot of liquid dye. When this has hardened, cut off pieces as you would from the commercial buds.

Mold Release

Some candlemakers say this isn't necessary. We disagree with them! It's a great deal easier to get a candle out of a prepared mold, so why make things difficult? Commercial mold release comes in spray cans and is sprayed on the inside of a mold.

We have found that salad oil works just as well. Rub a little on the inside of the mold, then rub it lightly with a clean paper towel to absorb any excess. If mold release is running down the inside of a mold in streaks, these streaks will show on the finished candle.

Scents

Entering a candle shop can actually make your eyes water from the array of perfumes used to scent the various candles. The days when the choice was bayberry, pine, or unscented is far behind us, and every exotic fragrance has been tried in candlemaking. Some are more successful than others, and many people still prefer unscented candles. But the aroma that assaults you as you enter a candle shop shouldn't be the basis for making a decision for scented or unscented candles. Most of those candles have a lovely smell when they stand alone instead of competing with each other.

If you choose to scent candles, use an oil-base perfume (one without any alcohol) or a few drops of perfume oil. We recommend that you use it sparingly. A subtle aroma is preferable to one that overpowers you. If you fail to put in enough to notice, you can still use the candle. But if you overdo it, the candle may be too objectionable to burn.

Pots, Pans, and Utensils

Among the kitchen utensils needed for candlemaking, three deserve particular mention—a double boiler or its equivalent, a candy thermometer, and a vessel with which to pour wax.

It is essential to have a large double boiler (wax expands when it melts) or a reasonable substitute. A large pot with an iron trivet on the bottom and a smaller pan or a coffee pot inside works well. Fill the large pot to the desired height with water; the water should come well up the sides of the coffee pot, but be sure that no water gets inside of the coffee pot or even on the pouring spout. Water can ruin candle wax. Then put the wax into the coffee pot, remembering to allow room for expansion. Do not cover the pot.

A candy thermometer is another absolute essential. Attach the thermometer to the inside of the coffee pot or melting pan so that you will be aware of the temperature of the melted wax at all times.

Have on hand a spouted vessel with which to pour wax. Anything with a wide enough spout will do. If you have used a coffee pot for melting, you can pour directly from it. If you have melted wax in a pan, a large Pyrex measuring cup will make a good pouring container.

Other utensils needed are listed in "Tools of the Candlemaker's Trade" at the end of this section.

PREPARING THE WATER BATH

A water bath will give your candles a fine finish. You may omit this step, but your candle won't have that professional look.

You should prepare the water bath container before you begin to make a candle. The container must be large enough to hold the candle mold surrounded by water—a plastic bucket works well. Put the mold you are planning to use into the bucket. Fill the bucket with water to within an inch below the top of the mold. Remove the mold and carefully mark the water level. Pour out the water.

A brick or other weight is often needed to weigh down the mold while it's in the water bath, so have it ready to use when needed. Whatever the weight is, it must be clean.

PREPARING THE WAX

Break a piece of wax from the large slab. The size depends upon the size of the candle you're about to make. One quarter of a 10- or 11-pound slab will make a quart-sized candle. Be generous in cutting the piece of wax—you can always save what you don't use, but if you're short on wax you won't be able to fill the candle mold. Cover the wax with a towel, and break it into pieces with a hammer. The towel will prevent the wax from flying around.

Put the pieces of wax into the container that you are using for a melting pot (coffee pot, top of double boiler, etc.). Put the container in hot water over medium heat. You may add more wax a little at a time, but be sure you leave a 2- or 3-inch allowance for expansion. Keep track of the temperature of the wax with the candy thermometer.

If you are using stearin, add it to the melted wax at this point (use a metal spoon to stir the wax).

If you are using crystals, put them in a pan, add a small amount of wax from the melting pot (about 1/4 cup) and heat over medium heat, stirring cautiously so as not to spill wax over the side of the pan. When the crystals have dissolved, remove the pan from the heat instantly and pour the mixture back into the melting pan. Be sure the heat is off under the wax when you do this.

Now add color. This step is one for experimentation. When the color is added to wax in a pot, it's difficult to tell what it's really going to look like in the finished candle. To test the color, drop a teaspoon of hot wax onto a piece of waxed paper. Let it dry. This hue will be close to the candle color, but expect the finished candle to be somewhat darker. If you think the color is too light, then add more color to your melting pot. If you think you've overdone it with the color, add more wax pieces and melt them into the colored wax.

When all the dye is melted, turn off the heat and remove the melting pot from the stove. Stir well to blend the color into the wax. If you're going to use scent, put it into the wax.

POURING THE CANDLE (METAL MOLDS)

Now you are ready to pour the wax into the mold. The process varies a little depending on the type of mold you're using. The instructions below are for using a purchased metal mold. Separate sections follow which describe variations of the procedure for making candles in molds found around the house, container candles, and hurricane candles.

Make sure that the mold is meticulously clean (dismantle it first), and put the mold together according to the instructions that came with it. Preheat the oven to 150°F (65°C).

Cut a piece of braided wick, of the width recommended on the instructions that came with the mold, about 6 inches longer than you need for the candle. Dip the piece of wick into hot wax. When the wax has cooled enough so that you can comfortably touch it, pull the wick straight with your fingers and let the wax harden on the wick. This will only take a minute or two.

Turn the mold upside down and you will see a hole in the bottom. Push the wick through this hole. Turn the mold right side up, and pull the wick up 4 inches above the top of the mold. Tie the top of the wick securely to a pencil balanced across the top of the mold.

Lay the mold on its side and pull the other end of the wick tightly through the bottom. The wick should be pulled taut, and the pencil held tightly against the top edge of the mold. Center the wick as you do this. Replace the screw in the bottom of the mold, winding the wick around the screw. Carefully seal the screw and wick hole with masking tape or chewing gum so that wax won't leak out of the mold.

Prepare the mold with mold release or salad oil. Place the mold into the preheated oven for a few minutes until it's hot. Remove with hot pads, and place it right side up on your work area.

Pour melted wax into a Pyrex measuring cup, coffee pot, or other spouted pouring vessel. Holding the metal mold in one hand (with hot pad) and the pouring vessel in the other, tip the mold and pour hot wax into it. Let the wax run down the side of the mold, and straighten the mold gradually as it fills until wax comes to 1/2 to 1 inch from the top. (Keep some melted wax. You'll need it later.) The wax is poured this way to prevent splashing and minimize bubbles.

After the mold has stood long enough to settle (about 3 minutes), gently tap the sides with the handle of a knife. This should disperse any bubbles that may have started to form in the candle.

In spite of your efforts to form a tight seal at the bottom of the mold, you may find that a little wax is leaking. In this event, put the bottom of the mold into a pan containing a little cold water. Leave it for a minute or two. This should make the wax congeal enough to prevent further leaking.

If you're using a water bath, fill the plastic container with lukewarm water up to the mark you made (see "Preparing the Water Bath," above). Gently lower the wax-filled mold into the water bath. Weigh down the top with a brick or other weight if the candle starts to float. Be careful—you must not get water inside the mold! When a fairly thick film has formed on the top of the wax, take the mold out of the water bath.

If you're omitting the water bath, just let the mold set until a thick film has formed on top.

If remaining wax in the melting pan has cooled, reheat it. With a pencil, make three holes around the wick, piercing the wax that has hardened. Pour melted wax into these holes. This fills in the air pockets which form when the cooling wax contracts.

As the candle cools and hardens, continue poking holes (only three each time) in the top layer and filling with hot wax. Do this three or four times. The wax right under the top of the candle will be the softest, so you should have no problem piercing through to soft wax.

In about 5 or 6 hours (depending on the size of the candle), the candle should be hard and cool. Now turn the mold upside down and remove the screw. The candle should slide from the mold when you do this. If it doesn't come out, try putting the mold in the refrigerator for an hour, then turning it upside down again. If it still doesn't come out, tap it lightly on the top and bottom (not the sides or you'll damage the candle). If you have used mold release, your candle should slide out. If none of these methods work (a rare occurrence), soak the mold in hot water to release the wax. And start over again.

After the candle has been released from the mold, you will notice a seam up one side. Shave this off with a sharp knife. Cut the wick on the bottom of the candle so that it's even with the wax. Cut wick on top of the candle to about $1/2$ inch in length.

The bottom of the candle will probably not be flat. You can level it with a cheese grater, or rub the bottom on a heated skillet (removed from heat) until it is level.

MOLDS FROM AROUND THE HOUSE

We think using various containers in interesting shapes found around the house is the most challenging and therefore the most fun. Your candles can be truly original works of art when you mold them in an artistic bottle or an odd-shaped gelatin mold. Be careful, though—some plastic containers may not withstand the heat of the wax.

Bear in mind, too, that if the top of the mold isn't the widest part of it, you're going to have to destroy the mold to remove the candle. We suggest starting with milk cartons and progressing to more exotic shapes. For many of these odd-shaped candles, you must insert the wick after the candle has been made. Never do this while your candle is still in the mold or the candle will crack. Remember that these improvised molds do best with a wax with a low melting point.

Prepare the wax as described earlier. Prepare the mold with mold release.

If you can insert the wick before the candle is poured, put in a cloth-covered wire wick weighted at the bottom with a small piece of chewing gum or a wick holder (sold especially for this purpose). Pour in about $1/2$ inch of wax to secure the wick in the bottom of the mold. When the wax has hardened, straighten out the wick and tie it tightly around a pencil balanced across the top of the mold. Center the wick.

Now pour melted wax into the mold and proceed as described above under "Pouring the Candle (Metal Molds)," eliminating the water bath, which is not effective with most improvised molds.

If you have not inserted a wick before pouring the wax, after you unmold the candle, heat an ice pick and carefully make a hole in the center of the candle, right to the bottom. Dip the wick in hot wax, straighten it when cool enough to handle, and insert it in the hole. Fill the hole around the wick with hot wax.

GLAZING

While candles made in metal molds and given water baths don't need to be glazed, candles made in homemade molds benefit from it. Glazing gives a smooth, hand-dipped finish to the candle. Glazing is done with hot wax to which no stearin has been added—you want the finish to be clear, not opaque. If your candle is white, you may want to glaze with a color.

The only equipment you need is a glazing container. A coffee can will often do for this purpose, but whatever is used must be slightly higher and wider than the candle to be glazed, and it must be able to hold hot wax.

Fill the glazing container with enough hot wax to cover the candle without overflowing the container. Hold the candle by the wick and dip it into the wax for a few seconds. Remove and let it dry thoroughly before trimming the wick and leveling the bottom.

CONTAINER CANDLES

Container candles are burned in the molds in which they're made. Glass molds are by far the finest for this purpose because they permit the flickering candlelight to shine through them. But the glass must be reasonably sturdy in order to be heat resistant.

To make container candles, you should use a wax with a low melting point. Neither stearin nor crystals are generally used. These candles are among the easiest to make.

After you have selected the mold (don't use mold release), insert a wick. Cloth-covered wire wick is appropriate, but it must be weighted at the bottom since there's no wick hole. You can use a small piece of chewing gum for this, or a wick holder. Insert the wick in the chewing gum, and tie the other end of the wick around a pencil, as you would if you were using a metal mold.

Warm the mold in a preheated oven. Fill the mold to within an inch of the top with melted wax. Set aside to cool.

When a fairly thick film has formed on top of the candle, make three holes around the wick with a pencil piercing the wax that has hardened. Pour melted wax into the holes. Repeat this step three or four times as the candle cools in order to fill the air spaces that occur as the wax cools and condenses.

When the candle is hard, trim the top of the wick so its about $1/2$ inch long.

HURRICANE CANDLES

Hurricane candles aren't really candles in the strict sense. They're wax shells to be set around votive candles. This gives a delightful, soft glow. Hurricane candles are best made in short, wide, metal molds with no wick hole in the bottom. You can also use cream cartons. Use wax with a high melting point, and do not use stearin. The process for making hurricane candles is the same as for any metal mold, up to the water bath stage—then proceed as follows:

Place the mold in the prepared water bath. When the wax has thickened to about $1/8$ to $1/4$ inch, cut the wax off the top of the candle with a knife and drain the liquid wax inside back into the melting pot. The thinner the shell, the more glowing the light shining through it. But the shell has to be able to support its own weight, so the taller you make a hurricane candle, the thicker the sides should be.

Before the wax shell gets really hard, cut around the bottom of the candle so that the bottom piece can be pushed out when the candle is unmolded. Since the mold is short and wide, you should have no trouble doing this with a long-handled knife. But take care not to damage the mold.

Turn the mold upside down on the newspapers in your work area so that any soft wax will drain off and the candle will slide from the mold. After the candle has been removed from the mold, you can push out the bottom piece of wax and even any ragged edges on the top or bottom of the shell.

Place the shell over a lighted votive candle.

TOOLS OF THE CANDLEMAKER'S TRADE

Here is a review of the equipment needed to make candles:

apron
pot holders
baking soda and large pan lid in case of fire
towel and hammer to break up wax
newspapers to cover work area
large double boiler or equivalent
candy thermometer
small pan to melt crystals in
spouted pouring vessel
large metal spoon
measuring spoons
waxed paper to test color on
candle mold
mold release or salad oil
scissors to cut wick
two pencils
masking tape or chewing gum, to seal bottom of metal mold
chewing gum or wick holder to secure bottom of wick, or
ice pick to poke hole for wick
sharp knife
bucket for water bath
brick or weight for water bath
glazing can

Not to mention the basics: wax and wick, plus stearin or crystals, dye, and scent, if you wish.

Insecticides, Repellents and Other Bugaboos

The cleanest of housekeepers occasionally has an infestation of some kind of crawling or flying pest. It's embarrassing, and it's a blue-ribbon nuisance, but some of these creatures are easily dealt with—often without the use of toxic substances that would be harmful to pets or children.

ANTS

Because some ants have wings, they are often mistaken for termites. Actually termites usually lose their wings when they take up residence indoors. Conversely, many people think these termites are ants because they "know" all termites have wings. It's really not difficult to distinguish between the two. Ants have small waistlines (just like the Gibson Girls) while termites have straight bodies with no indentation for a waist. Both species have wings in the rear as well as the front of their bodies. But the ants have small wings in the rear and larger ones in the front; the wings of a termite are of equal size. Although ants aren't as bad for your house as termites, they do build nests in rotting beams and other decaying woodwork, further weakening them. So along with their nuisance value, they aren't safe to have either in or around a house.

Many methods of ant control work without resorting to harmful chemicals. If ants are outside, and you're able to locate the ant hills, pour boiling water over them. Repeat this every day if you see any signs of activity. Some people swear that dish detergent added at a ratio of 1/4 cup for every gallon of water makes this boiling water remedy more effective.

Here's another antidote:

Sweet-Eating Ant Killer

1 tablespoon confectioner's sugar
2 tablespoons borax

Mix well and place in ant trails. This shouldn't be used near food, children, or pets—it's mildly toxic.

When a house seems overrun with ants and is also full of beloved children and pets, it's a problem finding the right insecticide. The entrance where ants come into a house from outside can be blocked with cinnamon (if you're successful in finding the spot where the ants are entering). These bugs seem to have an aversion to cinnamon and seldom will anything entice them to crawl through it.

Cucumber peels, left around where the ants are thickest, sometimes rid the house of the pests. Small red ants shy away from peppermint, and large black ones can be sent scurrying by sprinkling crushed catnip around (if the cat doesn't get there first).

Napthalene flakes are also quite effective at repelling ants. The flakes won't kill the ants, but they'll make them look for a new home. Use napthalene with caution. It's mildly toxic.

Here are two recipes for nontoxic ant killers. You don't have to be fearful of using either of these mixtures around the kitchen.

Sugar Bait

1/2 cup honey
2 tablespoons sugar
1/2 cup dry yeast

Mix ingredients together. Put the resulting paste around where the ants are troublesome. If possible, use a small plastic container with a cover, and pierce holes in it for the ants to enter (the sweetness of this mixture is apt to attract the family pet).

Spice Bait

1 tablespoon red pepper
1 tablespoon ground cloves
2 tablespoons boric acid powder

Mix ingredients together and place in ant trails.

BATS

These ugly, winged mammals frequently roost in attics, between walls, and under porches. Getting rid of them once they're firmly entrenched is a job that should be left to a professional exterminator. Fumigation may be the only answer. Don't attempt a confrontation with them yourself, because they're sometimes rabid.

There are ways to discourage bats, however. If you have an attic that bats might find attractive, sprinkle the floors and window sills with napthalene flakes or dichlorobenzene. Neither of these products will kill any bats that may be lurking around, but they will be encouraged to look elsewhere for shelter.

COCKROACHES

These pests are found more in older buildings than in new structures. They're more difficult to get rid of in brick buildings than in wooden ones because they lay their eggs right in the bricks. Many an immaculate apartment dweller has found, much to his or her dismay, that the kitchen is infested with cockroaches which have come from the apartment of a not-so-clean neighbor.

Cockroaches favor hiding places under a sink, behind a refrigerator, or in a darkened cabinet or closet. They slip into cracks in walls, and they love to run up and down water pipes, disappearing when you're looking for them. They can often be found on the bottoms of tabletops and chairs, on bookshelves and even in books. So these are the areas where insecticides will be the most effective. Here are a few remedies which aren't lethal to humans but should do in the roaches:

Roach Powder

5 tablespoons borax (this is slightly toxic)	1 tablespoon plaster of Paris
2 tablespoons arrowroot	2 tablespoons cocoa powder

Mix ingredients well, and put the powder in those out-of-the-way places. This powder which is useful against silverfish, too, should be left out for a few days after all signs of the bugs are gone. *Note:* Do not put plaster of Paris down the drain.

Cockroach Fizz

$^1\!/_2$ cup baking soda
1 tablespoon sugar

Mix together and put in roaches' hiding places. Roaches generally walk through the bait that's set for them, and then lick it off their feet. Since they can't digest the baking soda in this one, they explode.

Powdered alum and peppermint oil are both old-fashioned roach remedies, or you can whip-up this one that grandma used to make:

Cockroach Cocktail

1 teaspoon oil of eucalyptus
1 teaspoon oil of peppermint
1 teaspoon vanilla extract

Mix ingredients and leave in a shallow saucer, or use the solution to paint the edges of kitchen cabinets or the undersides of drawers.

FLEAS

A house full of fleas is a house full of misery! Here's how this problem usually comes to pass: female fleas lay eggs on the skin of your pet, and as your dog walks through the house wagging his tail and shaking, he spreads the eggs to carpets, furniture, and floors. When you're cleaning regularly, these eggs are scooped up in the vacuum cleaner and don't get a chance to develop in your home. But when you take a vacation, leaving the house closed up and the eggs undisturbed, you'll come home to a house that's literally jumping. Even after eggs have hatched, the first step in ridding your house of flea infestation is a thorough cleaning.

Chamomile flowers and fennel hair (or tops) strewn around the house will help rid the place of fleas. But if the bugs are really taking over, your best bet is a professional exterminator.

Fleas on animals present a special problem because you want to use something that won't harm your pet. There are several old folk remedies for this problem.

If you want your dog to have restful, flealess nights, insert a handful of the herb pennyroyal in the pillow or bed on which he sleeps. Fennel also can be tucked in with the regular stuffing with the same result. Here's a flea powder that is said to be very effective:

Pet Powder

2 tablespoons dried, ground pennyroyal
2 tablespoons dried, ground fennel
2 tablespoons cornstarch

Mix ingredients together well, and dust your pet with the powder. To get the maximum benefit, rub powder right into the skin.

FLOUR BUGS

These are the nasty little things that seem to appear in flour no matter how tightly you keep it covered. The problem can be solved before it happens by putting a dried bay leaf in the cannister with the flour. (It doesn't flavor the flour.) This is also a good practice with cereals.

FLIES

These bugs can ruin the best-planned picnic, and they're not much fun when they're buzzing around the living room, either.

Here's two good fly sprays that really get the job done.

Garlic Fly Spray

3 cloves garlic
2 tablespoons mineral oil
1 cup water
1 tablespoon detergent

Blend the garlic and mineral oil in a blender. Add water and blend again. Strain the mixture through cheesecloth, reserving the liquid and throwing away the bulk. Add detergent to the liquid, and store in a tightly covered jar.

When you want to spray for flies, mix 1 part of the garlic solution to 2 parts water, put in a spray bottle, and spray screens or outside areas where flies are troublesome.

Eucalyptus Spray

1 teaspoon oil of eucalyptus	1 cup alcohol
1 teaspoon oil of bergamot	½ cup water

Dissolve the oils in the alcohol. Add water and mix well. Spray outside or on screens to discourage flies.

FRUIT FLIES

Many fruits and vegetables, especially fresh from the garden, have tiny insects on them. Salad greens, herbs, and strawberries are particularly susceptible to this problem. To draw the bugs out, use salt or vinegar in the rinse water when you clean the produce. Then rinse again with clear water.

JAPANESE BEETLES

These dangerous bugs can crawl into someone's ear, and have actually been known to chew holes in eardrums. So if you're plagued with Japanese beetles, get rid of them! Oil of citronella should repel them, as it does most insects, but if you prefer to eliminate them completely, fill a small dish or a bottle cap with citral (oil of geranial). This fragrant oil is nontoxic to humans and pets, but it both attracts and kills Japanese beetles.

GARDEN PESTS

To keep your garden bug-free, it is best to use a nontoxic spray, especially on an herb or vegetable garden. We have found the following spray to be quite effective.

Nontoxic Herb Spray

3 cloves garlic	1 teaspoon liquid dish detergent
1 cup water	1 gallon water

Liquefy the garlic with the cup of water in a blender. Combine it with the detergent and the gallon of water. Let this ripen for 24 hours, then strain. Apply from a spray bottle as needed.

MOSQUITOES

The use of citronella candles outside can turn your mosquito-ridden patio into a bug-free place in a matter of minutes. You can make your own candles (see "The

Art of Making Candles"), adding a teaspoon of oil of citronella in place of the fragrant oil.

Smart country dwellers often plan their mosquito attack at planting time by putting in a row of tansy around the area they want to keep mosquito-free. This fragrant herb repels the pests.

Tansy can be dried and made into small sachet bags to be hung close to doors, windows, and other places that mosquitoes may enter. The Garlic Fly Spray also combats mosquitoes.

There are several concoctions that can be rubbed on skin to keep mosquitoes away:

Mosquito Repellent

$^1/_2$ cup glycerin
5 drops oil of eucalyptus
2 drops oil of rose

Blend ingredients together, and rub on skin. Remember that any aroma that's rubbed into pressure points is more noticeable because it radiates. This scent should be pleasant to humans but will definitely be offensive to mosquitoes.

Super Mosquito Repellent

$^1/_4$ cup U.S.P. grade mineral oil
2 teaspoons camphor
2 teaspoons oil of citronella

2 teaspoons oil of pennyroyal
4 drops oil of cloves

Mix together and apply to skin.

Simple Mosquito Repellent

1 teaspoon ammonia
$^1/_4$ cup rubbing alcohol

Mix together and apply to skin. This one is used in the kibbutzim in Israel.

In controlling mosquitoes, it helps to eliminate as many of their breeding places as possible. Since they breed in water, remove any containers from outside that may fill up with rainwater and attract them. If you have trees with large holes in them, fill the holes with concrete. Be sure that the rain gutters around your home are unclogged and free of stagnant water.

MOTHS

"Summertime and the livin' is easy" . . . at least for the moths, if you haven't taken proper steps. They'll be fat and happy feeding on your clothes.

The first step toward avoiding moths is to clean well—vacuum rugs, drapes, and furniture when it's moth season. Get at the places in carpeting where the furniture legs sit. Get down behind the cushions of overstuffed pieces. Vacuum in corners, around baseboards, and all the other nooks and crannies that attract moths. If you're thorough, you'll probably pick up most of the larvae or eggs in your vacuum cleaner. Be sure you empty the bag of your vacuum cleaner *outside*.

Clean garments before you store them away for the summer. Brush them well and hang them outside in the air. The sunshine will cause the eggs to fall off the clothes.

Store woolens and other goodies that moths are liable to attack in air-tight (or as near to it as possible) boxes, or in garment bags in closets.

Putting whole cloves, wrapped in cloth, in with your clothing will drive away moths. Or you can use napthalene flakes, but your clothes won't smell as nice. We like to pack winter clothes away with a moth-repelling, sweet smelling sachet:

Moth Sachet

1 tablespoon ground cloves	1 teaspoon thyme
¹/₂ tablespoon ground cinnamon	1 tablespoon dried, crushed lavender
1 tablespoon dried, crushed berga-	flowers (rose petals may be substi-
mot leaves	tuted)

Mix all ingredients together and sew into a sachet bag (see pages 126–127).

SPIDERS

Although most spiders are helpful because they eat other less desirable bugs and help maintain the delicate ecological balance that's been so threatened in the past few years, it's no fun to have a house full of them. Powdered sulfur, scattered around where they're liable to enter, will discourage them while still allowing them to live and perform their important function in nature.

Glues and Pastes:
A Sticky Subject

Some glues and pastes can be made from ingredients found in most homes. Others need only a few inexpensive ingredients to reproduce commercial brands.

For generations mothers have been making paste from flour and water. The formula is simple: add enough water to a cup of flour to make paste. Children can amuse themselves for hours with a stack of old papers, a pair of scissors, and a cup of paste. It's a great rainy day activity.

We find using condensed milk is an improvement on the flour and water paste. It's not as messy, it keeps better, and it doesn't become sour. You can use the milk for pasting right out of the can. When the pasting session is over, cap it tightly and store in the refrigerator for the next rainy day. It will keep almost indefinitely.

If you need a good all-purpose cement, try this:

Simple Cement

2 teaspoons glycerin
2 teaspoons water
1 teaspoon litharge (lead monoxide)

Mix the glycerin and water. Add litharge. If the paste isn't thick enough, add more litharge until it's the desired consistency. The only drawback to Simple Cement is that it must be used right away and can't be stored, so don't make a large batch.

China Cement

When you've broken one of your best china cups, try mending it with this strong mixture:

2 tablespoons beeswax
1/4 cup rosin

Melt beeswax in the top of a double boiler over low heat. Remove from heat and stir in rosin. Use immediately.

Glass Glue

Glass, paper, porcelain can be quickly mended with this:

1/2 cup casein powder
1/4 cup borax powder
hot water

Mix first two ingredients and make a paste by adding hot water. This may be stored in a tightly capped bottle or jar.

Book Paste

When the binding has come off a beloved book, don't despair! Mend it with this mixture:

2 teaspoons cornstarch	1 teaspoon borax powder
1 teaspoon dextrin	4 teaspoons glycerin
1/4 cup cool water	1 cup boiling water

Dissolve cornstarch and dextrin in cool water. Dissolve borax and glycerin in boiling water. Combine the two mixtures and store in a tightly lidded jar.

2
Foods

Homemade Baking Mixes:
Better Than Betty Crocker

Commercial baking mixes are multiplying like gerbils, and there is no end in sight! Every week, yet another bunch comes into view through a major advertising campaign. Apparently, consumers get tired of the same old flavors and need to be constantly stimulated by new taste thrills. If it was chocolate last week, this week it's chocolate mint or chocolate fudge or double chocolate. Next week we expect chocolate-almond-triple-fudge-with-mint-chips. Just remember that whatever they do in their experimental kitchens, you can do in yours. In fact, anything Betty Crocker can do, you can do better!

Mixes do save time, if not money, but, if you want to save *both*, you can make your own mixes on some quiet afternoon, ready to whip up baked goodies at a moment's notice. The jaded palate problem can be solved by jazzing up the basic recipes with an occasional substitution or addition. We definitely encourage using what you happen to have on hand. Some of the best dishes are discovered that way!

In the following recipes for homemade mixes, when eggs and shortening are to be added to the mix, it's best to have them at room temperature. If, like us, you sometimes decide at the last minute to bake, you can speed matters up by putting the shortening into a small bowl on the stove while other foods are cooking and there's hot steam hovering about. Or, if you have a gas range, you can put the bowl in the oven and the heat from the pilot light will soften the shortening. Eggs can be placed in a bowl of tepid water (not warm—you don't want to cook them!) for 15 to 20 minutes, enough to take off the refrigerator chill.

When beating egg whites separately, be certain not a speck of the yolk gets into the bowl or they won't whip up properly. If yolk gets into the egg whites anyway, carefully lift it out with an egg shell. Be sure, too, that the beaters are grease-free.

With homemade mixes, you have the best of both worlds—all the convenience of the ready-made, yet, if anyone asks, "Did you make this from scratch?" you can truthfully answer, "Yes."

HOMEMADE BISCUIT MIX AND WHAT
YOU CAN MAKE WITH IT

Biscuit Mix

6 cups sifted all-purpose flour, divided	3 teaspoons salt, divided
12 teaspoons baking powder, divided	³/₄ cup (1¹/₂ sticks) salted butter or shortening

Put 2 cups of the flour into a sifter, followed by 4 teaspoons baking powder and 1 teaspoon salt. Sift into a large bowl. Without moving the sifter, repeat the process twice more until all dry ingredients are sifted into the bowl. Stir lightly but well with a spoon. Slice the butter into the flour mixture. Using a pastry cutter or two knives, cut the butter into the dry ingredients until the mixture has the consistency of cornmeal. Store in a tightly covered container in the refrigerator until needed. Always stir before measuring.

Note: This recipe may be doubled, although it will be easier to use two bowls rather than one.

Baking Powder Biscuits

2¹/₂ cups Biscuit Mix
³/₄ cup milk

Preheat oven to 425°F (220°C). Pour milk into Biscuit Mix. Stir with a fork. Knead lightly in the bowl a few times to form dough. On a floured board, roll out the dough so it is ½ inch thick. Cut rounds with a biscuit cutter. Lay the rounds of dough on a greased baking sheet, and bake 15 minutes or until golden brown. *Yield:* 12 biscuits.

Cheese Biscuits

Add 3 tablespoons grated Parmesan cheese to dry ingredients in Baking Powder Biscuit recipe.

Onion Biscuits

Sauté ¹/₄ cup chopped onion in 1 tablespoon butter until onion is limp. Add to Baking Powder Biscuit dough.

Herb Biscuits

Add 1 tablespoon finely chopped fresh parsley, 1 teaspoon dried basil, and ¹/₂ teaspoon dried thyme leaves to dry ingredients in Baking Powder Biscuit recipe.

Shortcake

2¹/₂ cups Biscuit Mix
3 tablespoons sugar
³/₄ cup milk

Add the sugar to the Biscuit Mix. Add milk, and proceed as in Baking Powder Biscuits. When baked, split the biscuits, cover the bottom half with fruit sauce, add the top of the biscuit, more fruit sauce, and whipped cream.

Pecan Rolls

2 tablespoons butter
¹/₄ cup brown sugar, firmly packed
¹/₄ cup chopped pecans
¹/₂ teaspoon cinnamon

2¹/₂ cups Biscuit Mix
2 tablespoons granulated sugar
³/₄ cup milk

Preheat oven to 425°F (220°C). Melt the butter in a small skillet. Add brown sugar and stir over low heat until it is dissolved. Add pecans and cinnamon to sugar mixture. Set aside.

Stir the granulated sugar into the Biscuit Mix. Add milk, stir, and lightly knead the dough in the bowl. On a floured board, roll out the dough into a rectangle 1/2 inch thick. Spread pecan filling on the top. Roll up, jelly-roll fashion. Cut the roll into slices 1/2 inch thick, and place the slices in a well-greased baking pan. Bake 15 minutes or until golden brown. *Yield:* 12 rolls.

Franks in Blankets

Roll cocktail franks in small squares of Baking Powder Biscuit dough. Pinch dough together around frank. Bake at 425°F (220°C) until golden brown.

Chicken Pie

Top a chicken pie with rounds of Baking Powder Biscuit dough instead of with pastry. Bake at 400°F (205°C) until golden brown.

Beef Shortcakes

Split baked Baking Powder Biscuits and spoon on hot beef stew (without potatoes) and gravy. Try this using Herb Biscuits, too.

Baked Reuben

Combine corned beef, sauerkraut, and thousand island dressing in a casserole. Top with slices of Swiss cheese and ring the casserole with rounds of Baking Powder Biscuit dough. Bake at 400°F (205°C) until casserole is bubbly and biscuits are golden brown.

Pancakes

1 tablespoon lemon juice or vinegar	1 1/2 cups Biscuit Mix
1 cup milk	1 egg
2 tablespoons sugar	

Pour lemon juice or vinegar into the milk and set aside. Mix the sugar with the Biscuit Mix. Beat the egg and milk together. Pour liquid ingredients into dry ingredients, and stir with a fork. Do not overbeat. Bake the pancakes on a hot, lightly greased griddle (400°F [205°C], if you have a temperature-controlled griddle or frying pan).

Apple Pancakes

Add 1/2 cup coarsely grated raw apple (without peel) and 1/2 teaspoon cinnamon to Pancake batter.

Corn Fritters

1 egg	2 cups corn kernels
1/2 cup milk	deep fat for frying
1 2/3 cups Biscuit Mix	

Beat the egg and milk together. Stir liquid ingredients into the Biscuit Mix with a fork. Fold in the corn. In a deep fryer, heat fat to 375°F (190°C). Drop the batter by teaspoons into the hot fat and fry until golden brown on all sides. Do not pierce fritters with a fork. Lift out with a slotted spoon and drain on absorbent paper. Serve hot. *Yield:* 5 servings.

Clam Fritters

Follow the preceding recipe, substituting ¼ cup clam broth for half the milk and 1 cup chopped cooked clams for the corn, and adding 1 tablespoon minced fresh parsley.

Tea Scones

½ cup milk	¼ cup raisins, plumped
½ tablespoon lemon juice	2½ cups Biscuit Mix
2 tablespoons sugar	1 egg

Preheat oven to 425°F (220°C). Combine the milk and lemon juice and set aside. Stir sugar and raisins into the Biscuit Mix. Beat the egg and milk together. Now pour the liquid ingredients into the Biscuit Mix and stir with a fork. Lightly knead a few times to form dough. On a floured board, roll out the dough so it's ½ inch thick. Cut into circles or wedges. Place scones on a greased baking sheet, and brush them with milk. Bake 15 minutes or until lightly brown. Serve hot with butter and jam. *Yield:* 12 scones.

Apple-Cinnamon Coffee Cake

½ cup sugar, divided	3 tart apples, peeled and sliced thin
2 cups Biscuit Mix	1 teaspoon cinnamon
1 cup milk	1 tablespoon butter
1 egg	

Preheat oven to 425°F (220°C). Mix ¼ cup of the sugar with the Biscuit Mix. Beat the milk and egg together. Pour the liquid ingredients into the Biscuit Mix and stir with a fork. Spoon the batter into a greased 9-inch-square baking pan. Press the apple slices into the batter in rows, thin edges down. Sprinkle with remaining sugar and cinnamon. Dot with butter. Bake 25 minutes or until golden brown. Serve warm. *Yield:* 6 servings.

Dumplings

1 cup milk
2 cups Biscuit Mix

Pour the milk into the Biscuit Mix and mix with a fork. There should be at least 2 cups simmering liquid in the stew (or whatever mixture the dumplings are to be cooked in). Drop the batter by teaspoons into the stew. Cover and simmer 12 minutes without lifting cover. Dumplings should be puffed and dry inside. *Yield:* 6 servings. *Note:* Larger dumplings take 15 to 20 minutes to cook.

Dessert Dumplings

Add 2 tablespoons sugar to the Biscuit Mix in the preceding recipe. Cook dumplings in a fruit sauce.

HOMEMADE WHOLE WHEAT MIX AND WHAT YOU CAN MAKE WITH IT

Whole Wheat Mix

3 cups sifted all-purpose white flour, divided	3 teaspoons salt, divided
12 teaspoons baking powder, divided	3 cups whole wheat flour
6 tablespoons sugar, divided	3/4 cup powdered milk
	3/4 cup corn oil

Put 1 cup of the white flour into a sifter, followed by 4 teaspoons baking powder, 2 tablespoons sugar, and 1 teaspoon salt. Sift into a large bowl. Without moving the sifter, repeat the process twice more until all the dry ingredients except the whole wheat flour and the powdered milk have been sifted together. Add the whole wheat flour and dry milk. Stir lightly but well. Add the corn oil. Stir with a fork until completely blended.

Store in a tighlty covered container. Refrigerate in summer. Always stir before measuring.

Whole Wheat Biscuits

2 1/2 cups Whole Wheat Mix
2/3 cup water

Preheat oven to 425°F (220°C). Pour the water into the Whole Wheat Mix and stir with a fork. Knead lightly in the bowl to form dough. Roll the dough out on a floured board so it is 1/2 inch thick. Cut rounds with a biscuit cutter. Lay the rounds of dough on a greased baking sheet, and bake 15 minutes or until golden brown. *Yield*: 12 biscuits. Any of the biscuit variations may be used.

Whole Wheat Pancakes

1 3/4 cups Whole Wheat Mix	3/4 cup water
2 tablespoons sugar	1 egg

Stir the sugar into the Whole Wheat Mix. Beat the egg and water together. Pour liquid into the dry ingredients and stir with a fork. Do not overbeat. Bake the pancakes on a hot, lighty greased griddle (400°F or 205°C, if you have an electric griddle or frying pan).

HOMEMADE CAKE MIX AND WHAT YOU CAN BAKE WITH IT

Cake Mix

6 cups sifted cake flour, divided	1 1/2 teaspoons salt, divided
7 1/2 teaspoons baking powder, divided	3 3/4 cups sugar, divided
	3/4 cup powdered milk, divided

Put 2 cups of the flour into a sifter, followed by 2 1/2 teaspoons baking powder, 1/2 teaspoon salt, 1 1/4 cups sugar, and 1/4 cup powdered milk. Sift into a large bowl. Without moving sifter, repeat the process twice more until all the dry ingredients have been sifted together. Stir lightly but well. Store in a tightly covered container. Always stir and sift before measuring.

Golden Cake Layers

3¹/₂ cups sifted Cake Mix
2 eggs, separated
³/₄ cup water

1 teaspoon vanilla extract
¹/₂ cup soft butter or margarine

Preheat oven to 350°F (175°C). Measure the sifted Cake Mix into a large bowl. Make a well in the dry ingredients. Add egg yolks, water, vanilla, and soft shortening. Beat 4 minutes, scraping sides and bottom of bowl with a rubber spatula at least three times. In a separate bowl, beat the egg whites until stiff but not dry. Fold them gently into the batter. Pour the batter into two 8-inch layer cake pans, greased and lined with thin plain paper (grease the paper, too).

Bake 25 to 30 minutes, or until the cake bounces back when lightly touched and is dry inside (test with a foodpick). Cool the layers for 5 minutes in the pans, then turn them out onto wire racks to finish cooling. Remove the paper. Good with creamy chocolate frosting!

Spice Cake

Follow the preceding recipe for Golden Cake Layers, adding 1 teaspoon cinnamon and ¹/₂ teaspoon ground cloves to the Cake Mix.

Orange Snack Cake

2 tablespoons brown sugar
1 teaspoon grated orange rind
2 tablespoons finely chopped pecans or walnuts
dash of cinnamon

3¹/₂ cups sifted Cake Mix
2 eggs, separated
³/₄ cup orange juice (about 2 oranges)
¹/₂ cup soft butter or margarine

Preheat oven to 350°F (175°C). Mix brown sugar, orange rind, nuts, and cinnamon. Set aside. Measure the sifted Cake Mix into a large bowl. Make a well in the dry ingredients. Add egg yolks, orange juice, and soft shortening. Beat 4 minutes, scraping sides and bottom of bowl with a rubber spatula at least three times. In a separate bowl, beat the egg whites until stiff but not dry. Fold them gently into the batter.

Pour the batter into a greased and floured 9-inch by 13-inch baking pan. Sprinkle the brown sugar mixture on top of the cake batter. Bake 25 to 30 minutes or until the cake springs back when lightly touched and is dry inside (test with a foodpick). The cake may be cooled in the pan on a wire rack. No need to frost this!

Chocolate Cake

3 squares (3 ounces) unsweetened chocolate
¹/₂ cup butter or margarine
3¹/₄ cups sifted Cake Mix
3 eggs, separated

²/₃ cup water
1 teaspoon vanilla extract
¹/₂ teaspoon almond extract (optional)

Preheat oven to 350°F (175°C). In the top of a double boiler, melt the chocolate with the butter over hot water. Cool slightly. Measure the sifted Cake Mix into a large bowl. Make a well in the dry ingredients. Add egg yolks, water, and flavorings. Beat 2 minutes, scraping sides and bottom of bowl with a rubber spatula at least once. Add the cooled chocolate-butter mixture. Beat 2 more minutes, scraping sides again. In a separate bowl, beat the egg whites until stiff but not dry. Fold them gently into the batter.

Pour the batter into a greased angel food cake pan, the kind that separates into two parts. Bake 45 minutes or until the cake springs back when lightly touched and is dry inside (test with a foodpick). Cool the cake 5 minutes in the pan. Loosen the sides and around the center tube with a knife. Gently remove the cake from the pan and finish cooling on a wire rack. Try this cake with a coconut frosting.

Quick Fruit Cupcakes

1 cup berries OR 1 cup combination of chopped fruit and nuts	1 egg
2¹/₃ cups sifted Cake Mix	³/₄ cup water
	¹/₄ cup soft butter or margarine

Preheat oven to 375°F (175°C). Mix berries (or fruit and nuts) with 1 tablespoon of the Cake Mix. Put the remaining Cake Mix into a large bowl. Make a well in the dry ingredients. Add egg, water, and soft shortening. Beat 4 minutes, scraping sides and bottom of bowl with a rubber spatula at least three times. Fold in the berries.

Spoon the batter into a muffin pan lined with paper baking cups. Bake 20 to 25 minutes or until golden brown and dry inside (test with a foodpick). Cool 5 minutes in the pan. Remove cupcakes to finish cooling on wire racks. *Yield:* 12 cupcakes.

Convenience Foods:
Seasoned with Profit for Manufacturers

The watchwords on seasoned convenience foods are "read" and "compare." *Read* the labels on any of the plethora of seasoned products and *compare* their prices with the prices of the same products purchased in their unseasoned states. Notice what seasonings are used. Can they be worth the difference in price? How inconvenient is it for a cook to add salt, butter, herbs, or spices to the pot? Is it so difficult a task that one should be willing to pay over twice as much for ready-seasoned foods?

Unseasoned cracked wheat for wheat pilaf costs less than half as much as ready-seasoned wheat pilaf. The seasonings in the latter are listed as "onions, natural flavorings, salt, starch, garlic powder, and spices." You have to add your own butter and vegetables, if you wish them. To the unseasoned variety, we add chicken stock along with vegetables, oil, butter, and seasonings. It's easy, delicious, nutritious, and certainly cheaper!

This is not a unique analysis. Seasoned rice or noodles or rice-and-macaroni, seasoned vegetables, frozen omelets, packaged potatoes, and "help" for hamburger or tuna will boost your grocery bills without turning your family meals into gourmet affairs. Only your own creativity can do that!

What the food manufacturers have done is to take a staple food, add flavorings, and charge much more for it. Plain rice, for example, at current writing, costs about $1.60 for 5 pounds. *Six ounces* of seasoned rice with chicken flavoring and preservatives costs about 50¢. We wonder, when we see consumers eagerly buy these expensive manufactured products, if the day will come when it will be impossible to find plain rice in the supermarket.

If you're willing to add your own butter to frozen vegetables, instead of buying them in a prepared butter sauce, you'll save about 10¢ per 10-ounce package. That surely seems worthwhile to us. This is not to disparage frozen vegetables, which can be an excellent buy when fresh ones are not in season.

R.H.

As a general rule of thumb, for maximum eating pleasure and minimum expense, you are better off buying plain staple foods and adding your own seasonings. The following recipes are deliberately modeled after some of the convenience products presently on the market. Although we can't cover them all, we know that there isn't one in the supermarket it wouldn't profit you to make from scratch.

Wheat Pilaf

1 onion, chopped	2 cups chicken or beef stock (pre-
½ green pepper, chopped (optional)	pared bouillon may be substituted)
1 cup sliced mushrooms (optional)	¼ cup tomato sauce
¼ cup olive oil	pinch of ground thyme
2 tablespoons butter	pinch of turmeric
1 cup cracked wheat	salt to taste

In a medium-size skillet, sauté vegetables in oil 5 minutes or until they are softened. Remove them with a slotted spoon and reserve. Add butter to the pan; then add cracked wheat. Sauté wheat until it is golden and glossy.

In a saucepan, bring the stock to a boil and add the tomato sauce, thyme, turmeric, and salt. Simmer 5 minutes. Pour the stock over the cracked wheat. Cover and cook over lowest heat for 30 minutes. All the liquid should be absorbed. Remove cover, fluff with a fork, and let dry over low heat for 5 minutes before serving. *Yield:* 4 servings.

Note: Wheat pilaf can also be baked in a covered casserole for 40 minutes in a 350°F (175°C) oven. Then remove cover, fluff with a fork, and bake 15 minutes longer. Baked pilaf has a somewhat drier and nuttier taste.

Rice Pilaf

1 onion, chopped
2 tablespoons butter
1 cup raw rice (white or brown)
chicken stock or prepared chicken
    bouillon

pinch of sage
salt and pepper to taste

In a medium-sized skillet, sauté the onion in the butter. Add rice and sauté while stirring until the rice is golden and glossy. Substitute chicken stock for the amount of water recommended on the rice package for 1 cup raw rice. Add sage, salt, and pepper. Cover and cook the length of time specified on the rice package. Fluff with a fork and serve. *Yield:* 4 servings.

Note: Rice may be baked in a covered casserole in a 350°F (175°C) oven. Heat stock to boiling before adding it to the rice. Baking will take from 20 to 25 minutes longer than top-of-range cooking.

Spanish Rice

Sauté 1 chopped green pepper with the onion in the preceding recipe. Substitute 1/2 cup tomato sauce for 1/2 cup of the chicken broth. Top with more tomato sauce before serving.

Saffron Rice

Crush several threads of saffron between your fingers and add it to the hot chicken stock in the Rice Pilaf recipe.

Herb and Beef Rice

Substitute beef stock for chicken stock in the Rice Pilaf recipe. Instead of sage, use 1/4 teaspoon ground thyme and 1/2 teaspoon dried basil. When cooked, stir in 1 tablespoon minced fresh parsley.

Orange Rice

1 cup raw rice (white or brown)
1/2 teaspoon grated orange rind
2 tablespoons orange marmalade

1/2 cup raisins
1/2 cup chopped walnuts

Add orange rind, marmalade, and raisins to rice while cooking it according to package directions. Stir in walnuts after rice is cooked. *Yield:* 4 servings.

    This is a good side dish with chicken, but try it, too, as a stuffing for Rock Cornish hens.

Rice 'n Macaroni

Prepare either Rice Pilaf, Herb and Beef Rice, or Spanish Rice, with the following changes: mix 1/2 cup uncooked orzo (rice-shaped macaroni) with the raw rice, and add 1 extra cup stock to the cooking liquid.

Noodles Alfredo

1 pound medium-sized egg noodles or fettuccini, cooked according to the package directions
1/2 cup (1 stick) butter, cut into pieces
1/2 cup freshly grated Parmesan cheese
salt and pepper to taste
1/2 cup light cream
1 tablespoon minced fresh parsley

Drain the noodles and return them to the pan. Stir in butter until melted. Sprinkle with cheese, salt, and pepper. Toss to mix. Warm the cream and pour into the noodles. Stir to coat. Spoon into a warm serving dish. Sprinkle with parsley. *Yield:* 4 to 6 servings.

Note: Do not substitute packaged grated cheese for the freshly grated cheese. Pre-grated cheese is too dry and too flavorless to make this dish properly.

Noodles Romano

2/3 cup butter
1 cup canned Italian-style tomatoes, drained and crushed
1 pound broad egg noodles, cooked according to package directions
1/2 cup freshly grated Romano cheese
salt and freshly ground black pepper to taste
8 slices peppered ham cut into strips (optional)

Melt the butter in a small saucepan; add tomatoes and simmer 5 minutes. Return drained noodles to pot. Sprinkle with cheese, salt, and pepper. Toss to mix. Pour the butter-tomato sauce over noodles and mix. Spoon into a warm serving dish. If desired, top with strips of peppered ham. *Yield:* 4 to 6 servings.

Note: Do not substitute packaged grated cheese for the freshly grated cheese. Pre-grated cheese is too dry and too flavorless to make this dish properly.

Noodles with Tuna

2 6 1/2-ounce cans tuna, flaked
1/4 cup (1/2 stick) butter
1/2 cup chicken stock
1/2 onion, chopped
1/4 teaspoon pepper
1 tablespoon capers
1 pound broad egg noodles, cooked according to package directions
2 tablespoons chopped fresh parsley

In a medium-sized saucepan, simmer tuna, butter, chicken stock, onion, pepper, and capers for 5 minutes. Return drained noodles to pot; pour on tuna sauce and mix. Spoon into warm serving dish. Sprinkle with parsley. *Yield:* 4 to 6 servings.

Skillet Beef Italiano

1 pound ground beef
1 onion, chopped
2 tablespoons olive oil
1 28-ounce can Italian-style tomatoes
1 teaspoon dried basil
1/2 teaspoon dried oregano
1 tablespoon chopped fresh parsley
1/8 teaspoon garlic powder
1 teaspoon salt
black pepper to taste
1 pound medium-sized shell macaroni
1 10-ounce package frozen peas
grated Parmesan cheese

In a large skillet, fry loose ground beef until brown. Remove to a bowl with a slotted spoon; drain off fat from the skillet. In the same skillet, sauté the onion in oil until golden. Drain the tomatoes and save the juice for another use. Add the drained tomatoes to the skillet along with the basil, oregano, parsley, garlic powder, salt, and pepper. Simmer 20 minutes with cover slightly ajar for steam to escape. Stir occasionally and break up tomatoes.

Meanwhile, cook the macaroni according to package directions. Add the frozen peas to the tomato sauce. Cover and simmer until peas are cooked, 5 to 7 minutes (check to make certain sauce is simmering, because the frozen peas will cool it off). Add the beef to the tomato sauce and heat through. Put the cooked macaroni into a large serving dish. Pour the beef and tomato sauce on top. Pass the cheese at the table. *Yield:* 6 to 8 servings.

Note: Cubed eggplant or sliced zucchini can be used in place of peas. Cooking time will be longer.

One-Dish Chili-Beef

1 pound ground beef
1 onion, chopped
2 tablespoons corn or peanut oil
3 cups cooked or canned red kidney
   beans

1/2 cup water
1/8 teaspoon garlic powder
2 teaspoons chili powder

In a large skillet, fry loose ground beef until brown. Remove to a bowl with a slotted spoon and drain off fat from the skillet. In the same skillet, sauté the onion in oil until golden. Add beans, water, garlic powder, and chili powder. Taste to correct seasoning. Simmer 5 minutes. Add the beef to the chili sauce and beans. Heat through. Serve in bowls with crackers on the side. *Yield:* 6 servings.

Vegetables for Dieters

Cook any vegetable in well-seasoned stock instead of water. If desired, when the vegetable is drained, stir with 1 tablespoon of lemon juice and minced fresh parsley. Vegetables cooked this way are so flavorful they need no further enhancement.

Butter Sauce for Vegetables

1/2 cup vegetable cooking water
1/2 teaspoon cornstarch
1/2 teaspoon sugar

2 tablespoons butter
salt and pepper to taste
2 cups drained cooked vegetable

Thicken the cooking water with the cornstarch, stirring constantly over low heat. Add the sugar, butter, salt, and pepper. Add cooked vegetable and simmer 3 minutes longer.

Sweet-and-Sour Sauce for Vegetables

In the preceding recipe, substitute 2 tablespoons brown sugar for 1/2 teaspoon granulated sugar. Add 1 tablespoon vinegar.

Chinese Sauce for Vegetables

1 teaspoon cornstarch
2 tablespoons soy sauce
2 tablespoons dry white wine
   or sherry
1/2 cup vegetable cooking water

1 teaspoon cooking oil
1/2 teaspoon sugar
1/8 teaspoon garlic powder
pinch of ginger
2 cups cooked vegetable

Mix the cornstarch with the soy sauce and wine in a cup until the cornstarch is dissolved. Combine the cornstarch mixture and remaining ingredients in a small saucepan. Bring to a boil, stirring constantly. Lower the heat and simmer 5 minutes, stirring occasionally. Combine the sauce with the vegetable.

Vegetable Omelet

1 cup leftover cooked vegetable, drained (spinach, peas, tomatoes, or mushrooms are especially good)	2 eggs
	1 tablespoon water
	salt and pepper to taste
2 tablespoons butter or oil	grated Parmesan cheese
dash of garlic powder (optional)	

In a medium-sized skillet, heat the vegetable in butter or oil until it is sizzling hot; add garlic powder. Beat the eggs, water, and salt and pepper together. Pour the eggs over the vegetables and lower the heat. Loosen the edges of the egg with a spatula to allow uncooked portion to run underneath until all the egg is cooked. Flip the omelet over, if you wish. Slide the omelet onto warm plate. Sprinkle with cheese. *Yield:* 1 or 2 servings.

Scalloped Potatoes

4 or 5 large potatoes	paprika
2 cups White Sauce (recipe follows)	2 tablespoons butter
bread crumbs	

Preheat oven to 325°F (165°C). Butter a 2-quart casserole and fill it to 1 inch from the top with thin rounds of raw potato. Cover with White Sauce. Sprinkle with crumbs and paprika. Dot with butter. Bake 1 hour or until potatoes are tender. *Yield:* 6 servings.

White Sauce

1/4 cup (1/2 stick) butter	1 teaspoon salt
2 cups milk, divided	dash of white pepper
1/4 cup flour	

In a small saucepan, melt the butter and add 1 1/2 cups of the milk. Heat but do not boil. Combine the remaining 1/2 cup milk with the flour, salt, and pepper in a jar or a blender. Shake or blend until lump-free. Pour the flour mixture into the hot milk. Stir constantly over medium heat until the mixture bubbles and thickens. Reduce heat to low; simmer 5 minutes, stirring occasionally.

Potatoes Au Gratin

Add 1/2 pound cheddar cheese, coarsely grated, to White Sauce. Proceed as for Scalloped Potatoes.

Breaded Foods, Stuffings, and Croutons:
Fighting the Big Bread Rip-Off

A recent addition to the dazzling array of boxed convenience foods is a flavored crumb coating for meats. Chops or chicken pieces are shaken in this mixture, then oven-baked because "it's better than frying." This may be true, but you don't need to pay over 50¢ for 2⁷/₈ ounces of bread crumbs and spices plus a plastic bag when it's a cinch to make similar crumb coating mixes yourself at a fraction of the cost. We recommend preparing them in advance for easy after-work cooking.

For those who like stuffing better than potato, the best stuffings are home-made—they taste better, they cost less (a leading brand of stuffing mix sells at about 70¢ for 6 ounces), and they're easy to make. If you want to cook stuffings on the range top, you can just as easily do that—and a hundred other things—with savory homemade mixes.

Croutons for soups or salads can be toasted and seasoned in your own kitchen. Expect to save 60 to 70 percent of the cost of packaged brands.

Personally, we never have sufficient stale bread around to make all of these crunchy delights. If you don't either, use fresh bread, slowly toasted in a 150°F (65°C) oven. Or, after you have finished cooking something else in the oven, pop a baking sheet layered with fresh bread slices into the oven, turn off the heat, and don't open the oven door for several hours. The slices will be white but crisp, easy to crush for crumbs. A blender is the all-time fastest crumb maker and helps to mix in spices and herbs, too. If you don't have a blender, crush with a rolling pin.

Spicy Crumb Coating

¹/₂ cup fine bread crumbs	1 teaspoon paprika
2 tablespoons toasted wheat germ, or whole wheat flour	¹/₄ teaspoon ground thyme
	¹/₄ teaspoon ground sage
¹/₂ teaspoon salt	8 drops Liquid Smoke
pepper to taste	1 tablespoon corn oil

With a fork, mix the crumbs, wheat germ, salt, pepper, paprika, thyme, and sage. Drizzle on the Liquid Smoke and oil. Stir briskly until there are no lumps. *Yield:* enough crumb coating for 1 frying chicken or 8 pork chops.

Note: This recipe can be doubled or tripled, and the extra crumb coating stored in a tightly covered container until needed. Toss with a fork before using.

Italian Crumb Coating

¹/₂ cup fine bread crumbs	¹/₂ teaspoon dried basil
2 tablespoons toasted wheat germ, or whole wheat flour	¹/₂ teaspoon dried oregano
	1 teaspoon dried parsley
¹/₂ teaspoon salt	¹/₄ teaspoon garlic powder
pepper to taste	1 tablespoon olive oil

Proceed as for Spicy Crumb Coating.

Barbecue Crumb Coating

1/2 cup dry bread crumbs	1/2 teaspoon dry mustard
2 tablespoons whole wheat flour	1/2 teaspoon salt
2 tablespoons brown sugar	1/4 teaspoon garlic powder
1 teaspoon paprika	12 drops Liquid Smoke
1 teaspoon chili powder	1 tablespoon corn oil

With a fork, mix crumbs, wheat flour, brown sugar, paprika, chili powder, dry mustard, salt, and garlic powder. Drizzle on Liquid Smoke and oil. Stir briskly until there are no lumps. *Yield*: enough crumb coating for 8 pork chops or 1 frying chicken.

Note: This recipe can be doubled or tripled, and the extra crumb coating stored in a tightly covered jar. Toss with a fork before using.

Oven-Fried Chicken

1 2- to 3-pound frying chicken, cut into pieces
1/4 cup milk
1 recipe Crumb Coating (any flavor)

Preheat oven to 375°F (190°C). Wet the chicken pieces in the milk; shake off excess. Pour the Crumb Coating into a large plastic bag. Shake the pieces of chicken in the bag, two or three at a time. Lay the chicken pieces in one layer on a greased shallow baking pan, skin side up. Bake 40 minutes or until cooked through.

Barbecue Baked Pork Chops

8 pork chops
1/4 cup tomato juice
1 recipe Barbecue Crumb Coating

Preheat oven to 375°F (190°C). Trim fat from the chops. Wet the chops in the tomato juice and shake off excess. Pour the Crumb Coating into a large plastic bag. Shake the chops in the bag two at a time. Lay the chops in one layer on shallow roasting pan. Bake 40 minutes or until cooked through. (Very thick chops will take longer.)

Devilish Stuffing for Fish

1/2 cup (1 stick) butter	1/2 teaspoon salt
2 cups fine bread crumbs	1/8 teaspoon Tabasco sauce, or to
1/2 teaspoon dry mustard	taste
1 teaspoon Worcestershire Sauce	juice of 1 lemon

Melt butter in a large skillet. Add the remaining ingredients, except lemon juice, and blend well. Store tightly covered in the refrigerator or freezer until ready to use. Just before using, toss with lemon juice. *Yield*: 2 cups stuffing for 2 pounds of fish.

Herb Stuffing for Fish

1/2 cup (1 stick) butter	1/4 teaspoon dried tarragon leaves
2 cups fine bread crumbs	1/2 teaspoon onion salt
1 teaspoon dried parsley	1 teaspoon paprika
1/2 teaspoon dried thyme leaves	juice of 1 lemon

Proceed as in recipe for Devilish Stuffing.

Basic Stuffing for Chicken

3 cups cubed stale bread or oven-
crisped bread
1/2 teaspoon salt
pepper to taste
1 teaspoon ground sage
1 teaspoon dried marjoram
1/2 teaspoon ground thyme

2 tablespoons minced fresh parsley
1/2 cup (1 stick) butter
1 large onion, chopped
1 stalk celery with top, diced
3/4 cup chicken stock or prepared
chicken bouillon
1 egg, beaten

In a large bowl, combine the bread cubes with the salt, pepper, sage, marjoram, thyme, and parsley. Mix well. (At this point you may store the mixture in a tightly covered container for future use.) In a small skillet, melt the butter and sauté the onion and celery until limp but not brown. Combine with the bread. Heat the stock and drizzle it over the bread mixture, stirring until all the bread is moist but not drenched. Stir in beaten egg. *Yield:* 3 cups (enough for a 7-pound roasting chicken).

Note: For a turkey, double the recipe.

Giblet Stuffing

Simmer poultry giblets until tender. Chop and add to Basic Stuffing.

Fruit Stuffing

Use Basic Stuffing recipe, decreasing sage to 1/2 teaspoon and substituting 1 cup apples for 1 cup bread. Add 1/2 cup raisins and 1/2 cup chopped walnuts.

Chestnut Stuffing

Use Basic Stuffing recipe, decreasing sage to 1/2 teaspoon and substituting 2 cups boiled, shelled chestnuts for 2 cups bread. To prepare the chestnuts, cut an X in their shells, boil for 20 minutes, and shell while warm.

Range-Top Stuffing

Use ingredients in Basic Stuffing, omitting the egg. Mix the bread cubes, salt, pepper, and herbs in a large bowl. Melt the butter in a medium-sized saucepan, and sauté the onion and celery until tender but not brown. Add chicken stock (beef stock may be substituted). Simmer 10 minutes. Drizzle liquid over bread and seasonings until they are moist but not wet. Cover stuffing and keep warm for 5 minutes; fluff before serving.

Tomato Stuffing for Vegetables

Use Basic Stuffing Recipe, omitting sage and substituting 1 1/2 cups crushed canned tomatoes with juice in place of stock. Add 1 teaspoon dried oregano and 3 tablespoons grated Parmesan cheese. Use to stuff peppers or hollowed-out zucchini. Bake in 350°F (175°C) oven until vegetables are tender.

Croutons

3 cups cubed fresh bread
1/2 cup (1 stick) melted butter or olive oil
salt, pepper, seasonings, and/or grated cheese as desired

Preheat oven to 250°F (120°C). In a large shallow baking pan, combine the bread with butter or oil and seasonings. Bake, stirring occasionally, until croutons are quite crisp (about 1 hour).*Note:* Butter gives a nice flavor if croutons are going to be used right away. Oil keeps better if croutons are to be stored for use later. Keep in a tightly closed canister or jar.

Salad Dressings and Other Saucy Staples

Salad dressings, mayonnaise, mustard, catsup, tartar sauce, and other staples are cheaper to make than to buy. The homemade flavor is hard to beat, and most of them take less time to make than it takes to go to the store and purchase them. With all these pluses, we don't understand why everyone doesn't create their own staples.

Old-Fashioned Mayonnaise

Mayonnaise, in its infinite varieties, is the basis for many good salad dressings. It's so easy to make with a blender that you can have a fresh batch weekly in just minutes. If you don't have a blender, you can use an electric beater—it will only take you a trifle longer. When making mayonnaise, have all the ingredients at room temperature before you begin. Use corn oil or any salad oil with a mild flavor.

1 egg	2 tablespoons lemon juice
1/4 teaspoon salt	1 cup oil (approximately)

Put the egg, salt, and lemon juice into a blender container and blend briefly (or beat well with electric mixer) until the mixture is golden. Through the opening in the top of the blender cover, add the oil very, very slowly, a few drops at a time, blending constantly, until you have used about half of the oil.

Add the remaining oil a bit faster (in a slow stream), blending constantly, until the mixture is thick and smooth. This takes about two minutes in a blender, or several minutes with a mixer. Add oil until the mixture will absorb no more.

The mayonnaise will be pourable when you are done mixing it, but after it is stored in the refrigerator in a covered glass jar, it will thicken considerably. If the mayonnaise should separate, return it to the blender or beat it with a mixer for a few seconds. *Yield:* 1½ cups

Note: 1 or 2 teaspoons of Dijon mustard, a dash of white pepper, and a dash of sugar may be added before you start blending in the oil if you prefer mayonnaise with a bit more bite. If you're using the mayonnaise as the basis for other dressings, however, it's best to omit these ingredients.

Mustard

This mustard is delicious!

1 tablespoon dry mustard	1/4 cup heavy cream
water	salt and pepper to taste

Mix the mustard with just enough water to form a paste. In a medium-sized mixing bowl, whip the cream until stiff. Fold the mustard into the cream and store in a covered container in the refrigerator. *Yield:* ¹/₂ cup

Tomato Catsup

Here's one thing you can do with that bumper crop of tomatoes:

25 pounds peeled, seeded tomatoes	¹/₂ tablespoon dry mustard
1 quart vinegar	1 teaspoon white pepper
2¹/₂ to 3 pounds of sugar	¹/₂ teaspoon cinnamon
1 tablespoon salt	¹/₂ teaspoon celery seeds
1 teaspoon paprika	1 teaspoon onion powder
¹/₄ teaspoon cayenne pepper	

In a large enamel or stainless steel kettle or pot, simmer the tomato pulp until it's reduced to a thick sauce (about 2 hours). Stir occasionally. In a medium-sized saucepan, heat the vinegar, and then stir in the sugar and salt until dissolved. Add the remaining ingredients and mix well. Slowly add the vinegar mixture to the tomato pulp, stirring constantly. Continue to simmer until the mixture reaches the desired consistency. Stir frequently. Remove from heat and bottle in sterile jars or put in small plastic containers for storage in your freezer. *Yield:* about 4 quarts

Anchovy Dressing

This is tasty served over a salad of crisp greens, hard-boiled egg slices, and croutons.

¹/₂ cup salad oil	3 fillets of anchovy, mashed
¹/₄ cup wine vinegar	pepper to taste

Mix all ingredients well, cover, and store in refrigerator. *Yield:* about 1 cup.

Apple-Horseradish Sauce

This sauce adds pizzaz to roast pork or pork chops.

¹/₄ cup grated horseradish
1 cup applesauce

Stir ingredients together. Store tightly covered in the refrigerator. *Yield:* 1¹/₄ cups.

Avocado Dressing

Serve this over a tossed green salad or a raw vegetable salad. It's also excellent with cold roast beef.

1 ripe avocado, peeled and mashed	¹/₄ teaspoon Worcestershire sauce
¹/₂ cup sour cream	¹/₂ teaspoon salt
¹/₄ cup Old-Fashioned Mayonnaise (see above) or commercial mayonnaise	

In a medium-sized mixing bowl, mix all ingredients together well. Store in a tightly covered glass jar in the refrigerator. Yield: about 1 cup.

Barbecue Sauce

This is good for either chicken or beef. If the meat is to cook for more than half an hour, don't baste it until the last 30 minutes of cooking time. This way you'll avoid a bitter taste that can occur with overcooking the sauce. If the meat is to cook less than 30 minutes, marinate it in the sauce before cooking.

1 cup Tomato Catsup (see above) or commercial catsup	4 drops Tabasco sauce
	$1/8$ teaspoon salt
$1/4$ cup lemon juice	$1/8$ teaspoon paprika
1 teaspoon brown sugar	$1/8$ teaspoon ground ginger

Combine all ingredients in a small saucepan. Simmer over medium heat for 10 to 15 minutes, stirring constantly. *Yield:* 1 cup.

Cherry Dressing

1 8-ounce package cream cheese	8 maraschino cherries, chopped
cherry juice from bottle of maraschino cherries	1 cup sour cream

Let the cream cheese stand for 15 minutes at room temperature and then mix in enough cherry juice to make the cheese soft. Mash the cheese till it's smooth, and add the sour cream. Mix in the cherries, and serve over a tart fruit salad. *Yield:* about 2 cups.

Citrus Dressing

1 cup Old-Fashioned Mayonnaise (see above) or commercial mayonnaise	$1/8$ teaspoon grated orange rind
	$1/8$ teaspoon grated lemon rind
	$1/8$ teaspoon grated lime rind
1 cup yogurt (for homemade, see page 87).	$1/2$ teaspoon sugar (more, if you have a sweet tooth)

In a medium-sized mixing bowl, blend the mayonnaise and yogurt together with a fork. Mix in the citrus rinds and add sugar to taste, stirring until the sugar has dissolved. Store tightly covered in the refrigerator. Use on fruit salad. *Yield:* 2 cups.

Creamed Horseradish Dressing

$1/4$ cup grated horseradish
$1/2$ cup sour cream

Mix together and serve with beef. This may be made milder or stronger according to personal preference using less or more horseradish. *Yield:* $3/4$ cup.

Creamy Cole Slaw Dressing

1 cup Old-Fashioned Mayonnaise (see above) or commercial mayonnaise	2 teaspoons sugar
	2 tablespoons cider vinegar
	1 teaspoon celery salt

Mix all ingredients together well and blend into your favorite slaw. *Yield:* about 1 cup.

Cucumber Dressing

This is good served with seafoods.

1/2 cup pared, finely chopped cucumber

1/2 cup Old-Fashioned Mayonnaise (see above) or commercial mayonnaise

1/4 cup lemon juice

1/8 teaspoon salt

1/2 cup sour cream

1/2 teaspoon dried dill

Mix all ingredients together well and store tightly covered in the refrigerator. *Yield*: about 2 cups.

French Dressing

1 cup olive oil

1/4 cup lemon juice

1 teaspoon sugar

1/2 teaspoon dry mustard

1 teaspoon salt

1 teaspoon Worcestershire sauce

dash of pepper

1 teaspoon paprika

1 clove garlic

In a medium-sized bowl, combine all ingredients, except garlic, and blend together well with a wire whisk. Add the garlic, and store in a tightly covered jar in the refrigerator. After a day or so, remove the garlic and discard it. Shake well before using. *Yield*: 1 1/4 cups.

Fruity French Dressing

This one is elegant on fruit salads.

1 cup corn oil

1/4 cup orange juice concentrate

1/4 cup pineapple juice

1 tablespoon lemon juice

1/4 cup sugar

1 1/2 teaspoons paprika

Whirl all ingredients in blender just long enough to mix. *Yield*: 1 1/2 cups.

Garlic Dressing

1 cup Old-Fashioned Mayonnaise (see above) or commercial mayonnaise

1/2 cup corn oil or other mild salad oil

2 tablespoons white vinegar

3/4 tablespoon salt

1 clove of garlic, minced

1/2 teaspoon dry mustard

Mix all ingredients well, and refrigerate in a tightly covered container. *Yield*: about 1 1/2 cups.

Gourmet Tartar Sauce

1 cup Old-Fashioned Mayonnaise (see above) or commercial mayonnaise

3 gherkin pickles, minced

1/4 teaspoon garlic powder

2 teaspoons capers

2 teaspoons grated onion

1 teaspoon prepared mustard

1 teaspoon lemon juice

1 teaspoon sugar

salt and pepper to taste

1 tablespoon minced parsley

In a medium-sized mixing bowl, blend all ingredients well with a fork. Put in a covered container and refrigerate. *Yield*: 1 1/2 cups.

Italian Dressing

1 cup olive oil
1/4 cup wine vinegar
1/2 teaspoon salt
1/2 teaspoon pepper
1/4 teaspoon crushed dry basil

1 teaspoon crushed dry oregano
1 teaspoon crushed dry parsley
1/4 teaspoon dry mustard
1/4 teaspoon garlic powder

Put all ingredients in a glass jar that has tightly fitting cover. Shake well and refrigerate. *Yield*: about 1 1/4 cups.

Roquefort Dressing

No one will ever guess from the scrumptious taste how easy this cheese dressing is to make.

1 cup Old-Fashioned Mayonnaise (see above) or commercial mayonnaise
1 cup sour cream
1/4 pound crumbled Roquefort cheese

Mix well and refrigerate tightly covered. *Yield*: about 2 cups.
Note: If you like a stronger cheese taste, use 1/2 pound of Roquefort.

Russian Dressing

The French and Italians aren't the only ones with a taste for delicious salads.

1 cup Old-Fashioned Mayonnaise (see above) or commercial mayonnaise
1/2 cup Tomato Catsup (see page 79) or commercial catsup

1 teaspoon celery seeds *or* 1/2 teaspoon celery salt
1/8 teaspoon ground thyme

Mix all ingredients together thoroughly. Refrigerate in a covered container. *Yield*: 1 1/2 cups.

Sour Cream-Mayonnaise Dressing

Sour cream and mayonnaise, mixed in equal amounts, make a refreshing topping for fruit and gelatin salads.

Sweet and Low Dressing

Watching your weight? This is a delicious low-calorie salad dressing that is as good on tossed greens as it is on fruit.

1/2 cup cottage cheese
1/2 cup fruit juice

Blend ingredients well. Refrigerate in a tightly covered container. *Yield*: 1 cup.

Thousand Island Dressing

1 cup Old-Fashioned Mayonnaise (see above) or commercial mayonnaise
1/4 cup Tomato Catsup (see above) or commercial catsup

2 hard-boiled eggs, finely chopped
1 small onion, minced
1/4 cup minced sweet pickle or green olives
1/4 teaspoon garlic powder

Mix all ingredients together and refrigerate in a tightly covered container. *Yield:* about 1¹/₂ cups.

Cheese:
The Hard and Soft of It

Almost everyone likes some kind of cheese! This delectable dairy product appears in so many varieties, with such diversified flavors, odors, and textures that there is a cheese to suit the most discriminating palate.

Cheese is usually made from the milk of cows, goats, or sheep. Each one has a distinct and individual flavor, and the flavor will vary depending on what the animal has been eating too. Cheese can also be made from the milk of a host of other animals. Even buffalo or reindeer milk can be turned into cheese.

The cheese world consists of whole-milk cheeses, skim-milk cheeses, and cheeses made from partially skimmed milk; of soft cheeses, hard cheeses, and semisoft cheeses; and of ripened cheeses (those that have been aged) and those that are unripened (consumed soon after they are made). The main difference between hard and soft cheeses comes in the pressing stage of cheesemaking. The longer a cheese is pressed and the heavier the weight used in pressing, the harder the cheese will be. A well-pressed cheese is very hard and will keep for many months, although it can also be eaten immediately. The longer you age hard cheese, the sharper the flavor will become.

Gourmet cheese fanciers are called *turophiles*, and turophiles not only know what tastes good, they know what's good for them. Cheese, a beautiful and versatile food, is also incredibly nutritious. Ounce for ounce, cheese contains seven times as much protein as the milk from which it's made. It is rich in minerals, vitamin A, and, when made from whole milk, in milk fat. Hard and semisoft cheeses have more calcium than their softer counterparts, but soft cheeses make up for this deficit by providing more B vitamins.

Unfortunately, many of the cheeses available in this country today are processed cheeses. (The term alone is enough to dismay any true turophile.) These products are made from a blending of inferior natural cheeses. First they are shredded, and then they are heated until all the natural bacteria, which make cheese so lovely, have been destroyed. Natural cheeses mature slowly, through enzymatic action, while processed cheeses are made quickly, using extremes of heat to speed up the action and quantities of air to increase their volume. Since processed cheese is lifeless, it keeps almost indefinitely. This is its only advantage over natural cheese, and we consider it a small advantage—the majority of natural soft cheeses keep for at least two weeks in the refrigerator, and many hard cheeses will keep well over a year.

Most cheese should be kept tightly wrapped, in moisture-proof, air-tight wrappers. Cheeses such as Roquefort or bleu are exceptions to this. These "moldy" cheeses need to breathe a little and should be kept in almost air-tight containers. Ideally, hard cheese should be kept at 60°F (15°C). Since this is not feasible in most homes, the next best place is the bottom shelf of the refrigerator. But be sure to bring ripened cheese to room temperature before serving. Otherwise, you won't get the full benefit of the fine flavor. Soft unripened cheeses, such as cottage cheese, should be stored in the coldest part of the refrigerator and served cold.

If you notice a mold on the outside of hard or semisoft cheese, scrape it off and use the cheese. This is not an indication that the cheese has gone bad—it's simply the result of moisture.

Contrary to what you may have heard, there is no reason why cheese can't be frozen. It keeps well this way, and freezing doesn't destroy any of the nutritional value. However, it does slightly alter the texture of hard cheese, and you may prefer to use it for cooking or grating after it has been frozen. Never refreeze cheese once it has been defrosted.

Grate cheese just before you use it, it will dry out if you store it grated. You can use your blender for this, or grate by hand using a conventional grater.

CHEESEMAKING UTENSILS

You don't need anything fancy or expensive to make cheese—just a few basic things, most of which you have or can find around your home. Here they are:

A *large double boiler* is a must. This can be improvised from a 4-quart and a 6-quart pan. For making hard cheese, you will need even larger containers, namely one that holds 16 quarts and one that holds 20 to 24 quarts. We put milk in the smaller pan, place it in the larger one, and fill the larger one about 3/4 full of warm water. The large pots used for canning are good choices for this, if you have them—they run as large as 36 quarts and facilitate making large batches of cheese.

A *thermometer* is another essential. Any one that can be immersed in liquid (such as a candy thermometer) will do, but a floating dairy thermometer is the best choice.

Cheesecloth is needed to drain the curds and, if you're making hard cheese, to line the cheese form and wrap the cheese in. You will need about two yards for this.

A *colander* is extremely handy for draining the cheese. Since they're not expensive, we recommend purchasing one if you don't have one already.

A *long-bladed knife* is needed for cutting the curd; it should be able to reach down through the curd to the bottom of the pot. A *spoon* with an extra-long handle is a must, so that you can reach the bottom of the cooking container easily.

A couple of *large bowls* should be ready to drain the whey into and to hold the curd.

The equipment listed above is standard for making all kinds of cheese. But to make hard cheese, you need three more things: a cheese form, a "follower," and a weight or cheese press.

A *cheese form* can be easily made by punching several nail holes in the bottom of a 2-pound coffee can. The holes should be punched from the inside out to avoid ragged edges that will tear the cheese.

A *follower*, which fits inside the cheese form and sits on top of the cheese, can be made from a piece of wood about 1/2 to 1 inch thick. It should be cut to fit snugly but not tightly inside the coffee can or whatever form you are using, so it can move up and down as needed.

A *cheese press* can be purchased, but it really is an unnecessary expense unless you intend to make cheese frequently. Six or seven bricks, weighing 3 to 4 pounds each, will serve the purpose.

INGREDIENTS OF CHEESE

Cheese is made from milk, starter, and salt. The milk may be whole, skim, or made from nonfat dry milk. It may be either raw or pasteurized. If raw, milk for cheesemaking should be from an animal that has not been treated with any form of antibiotic for at least a week. Antibiotics do something to milk that prevents it from developing the acid content necessary for cheesemaking. Whatever milk you use should be brought to room temperature before you begin working with it.

The starter can be buttermilk, yogurt, or a commercial starter. We prefer buttermilk. You also need salt. Table salt will suffice, but flake salt is better because it is absorbed more quickly.

Rennet or rennin, which comes from the stomachs of animals, is often used in cheesemaking. It does speed up the process a bit, and it lends an acidic taste to the product, but we don't use it in our recipes. Since it is an animal product, many cheese-loving vegetarians are put off by cheese made with rennet, and we prefer the taste of cheese made the old-fashioned way.

Cottage Cheese

Soft, unripened cheeses are easier to make than hard cheeses, and cottage cheese is a good choice for beginners. If it's made with skim milk or nonfat dry milk, it will be similar to pot cheese. If you prefer to use whole milk, the end product will be more like ricotta.

$^1/_2$ gallon skim or whole milk or nonfat dry milk made according to package directions
1 cup buttermilk, for starter
salt to taste

Pour the milk into a 4-quart pan. Slowly heat it until it reaches 86°F (30°C) on dairy thermometer. Mix in the starter thoroughly. Cover the pan and set it in a warm place overnight or until the curd forms and whey (liquid) rises to the top.

With a long-bladed knife, cut the curd into $^1/_2$- to $^3/_4$-inch cubes. Insert the knife to the bottom of the pan with each cut (see figure). When the top of the curd looks like a checkerboard, insert the knife at an angle and cut the long cubes as well as possible. Drain the whey through a colander into a jar and save it.

Set the pan in a larger pan (6 quarts will do nicely) of warm water. Heat slowly, stirring frequently, until the curd reaches temperature of 106° to 110°F (41°–43°C). Continue to cook, maintaining this temperature, for about half an hour, until curds are quite firm. Stir often during this time, moving the curds on the inside to the outside edge of the pan so that they will heat evenly.

R.H.

Pour the curds into a colander lined with cheesecloth. Reserve the whey. Drain the curds for 5 minutes; then wrap the cheesecloth around the curds and rinse under cool water. Drain another 5 minutes again, this time discarding the runoff.

Salt the cheese to taste, and chill it thoroughly before serving. It will keep one to two weeks in the refrigerator. *Yield:* 2 cups.

Note: A few tablespoons of heavy cream may be worked into the cheese before chilling if you prefer a rich-tasting cheese. If, on the other hand, you're on a diet, use skim milk to make cheese, and do not add the cream.

Hard Cheese

10 quarts whole milk
2 cups buttermilk
1 tablespoon salt

In a large pot, placed in an even larger pot of warm water, heat the milk over medium heat until it is 86°F (30°C) on a thermometer. Remove from heat, taking the milk container out of the warm water. Thoroughly mix the buttermilk into the warm milk. Cover lightly and let stand at room temperature for 24 hours or until the milk has begun to form a curd and there is a watery whey on top.

With a long-bladed knife, cut the curd into 1/2 to 3/4-inch cubes. Insert the knife to the bottom of the pot with each cut so that cubes will be fairly uniform. When top of curd looks like a checkerboard, insert the knife at an angle and cut the long cubes as well as possible.

Stir the cubes or curds carefully. Now place the pot containing them into a larger pot of tepid water. Heat very slowly, stirring so that curds in the center are moved to the outside and vice versa. This is so that all the curds will heat evenly and be done at the same time. While you are doing this, raise the heat under the pot very slowly, a little at a time. It should take about half an hour for the curds to register 100°F (38°C) on the thermometer.

Keep the curds at 100°F (38°C), adjusting the heat under the pot as necessary, until a small amount of the substance breaks apart readily when you squeeze it between your fingers. Stir occasionally during this step, and don't be discouraged if the curd isn't ready for an hour.

Remove the pot from the heat and strain off the whey through a cheesecloth-lined colander into a large bowl. Reserve the whey. Tie the four corners of the cheesecloth together around the curds, and hang it on the kitchen faucet or other convenient place until the remainder of the whey runs off. This takes about half an hour.

Put the curds in a large bowl and stir gently to separate those which may be sticking together. Sprinkle salt over the curds, mixing it in while you do so that it will be evenly distributed and dissolved.

Line the bottom and sides of the cheese form with cheesecloth. Check the curd with the thermometer. When it registers 85°F (30°C), place the curd in the lined cheese form. Fold the cloth over the top of the curd. Place the round follower over the curd in the cheese form. Place two bricks on end, on top of the follower. Let it stand for 10 to 15 minutes (some whey will run out the bottom of the cheese form).

Remove the bricks and follower, and drain the cheese form. Replace the follower and bricks. This time add another brick. Keep adding a brick about every 5 minutes until you have used six or seven bricks. Some of them will have to be put lengthwise on top of the bricks which are standing on end. Allow the curd to stand this way for about an hour.

Remove the bricks and follower and drain off the whey. Turn the form upside down to remove the whey. Remove the cheese. (You may have to tug a bit at the ends of the cheesecloth before cheese slides out.) Carefully remove the cheesecloth from the cheese and dip the cheese into lukewarm water. This will remove any excess fat that may have been squeezed to the surface.

Cut a clean piece of cheesecloth, long enough to roll around cheese with a 2-inch overlap and with a 2-inch allowance on either end. Cut a circular piece of cheesecloth for each end of the cheese. Return the cheese to the cheese form. Replace the follower and bricks and let stand for 24 hours.

Again, carefully take the cheese out of the cheese form. Remove the cloth, and wipe the cheese dry with a clean piece of cloth. Examine the cheese thoroughly for any cracks or tears and gently smooth over any of these imperfections by dipping your fingers in hot water and working the cheese until it seals. Wash the cheese in warm water and wipe again with a clean, dry cloth.

Place the cheese in a very dry, cool (about 60° F or 15° C), clean place for four or five days. Wipe excess moisture from the cheese daily. During this process a rind should be forming on the cheese. If at the end of five days there is no sign of a toughening on the outside of the cheese, the spot you have chosen to put it in is probably not dry enough. Select a drier place, and proceed with this step until a rind has formed.

Wrap the cheese tightly in a plastic bag for storage and return it to the cool, dry place for aging. You may eat this cheese at any time, but the aging process will improve the flavor. It can be aged from six weeks to six months depending on the sharpness desired. The longer the cheese is aged, the sharper it will become. *Yield:* 2-2¹/₂ pounds.

Now that you've made hard cheese and found it's not really difficult, experiment. A different kind of milk, another starter, more or less pressure for a shorter or longer period, and more or less aging time will all affect the finished product to some degree.

It's very satisfying to serve wine and cheese and be able to say, "I made the cheese."

Whey

The whey that we urge you to keep and use is one of the world's most ignored and least expensive sources of nutrition. It contains lactose, lactalbumin, and most of the minerals present in milk. Because of the lactose, whey is considered a wonderful aid to digestion. Despite this, American dairy men throw out about 9 billion pounds of whey annually.

You can use whey to add nutrients to soups and stews, or you can make refreshing drinks with it. A glass of whey blended with a teaspoon of sugar and a few strawberries is a delightful summer drink. You can use other fruits and flavorings, too. Experiment and see what concoctions you can invent using whey as an ingredient.

Yogurt

This delightful dairy product—a cultured milk, not really a cheese—has become a real favorite. It's great for anyone who's watching calories, it aids digestion, and it's easy to make. A quart of milk will make about a quart of yogurt, which means store-bought yogurt costs three to four times more than homemade.

Yogurt is versatile—that's one reason why we find it so indispensable. It can be flavored with fresh fruit, vanilla, or a little instant coffee. It's also delicious mixed with cold vegetables for a salad or used as a dressing over diced cucumbers.

If you're not a calorie watcher, add a teaspoon of jam or jelly to a cup of fresh yogurt.

You need yogurt to make yogurt, because it's a living bacteria. So the first time you try this recipe, you'll have to purchase a container of plain, unpasteurized yogurt at the store, or you can buy yogurt starter from almost any health food store. From then on, use a bit of your own homemade yogurt for the starter.

Because homemade yogurt is preservative-free, it will keep just about a week, so only make what you will consume in that time.

> 1/2 cup nonfat, non-instant milk powder
> 1 quart milk
> 3 tablespoons yogurt or yogurt starter

In the top of a double boiler, mix the milk and milk powder with a wire whisk. Heat the milk just under boiling point. Remove the milk from the heat, and let the milk cool at room temperature for about 20 minutes until it's lukewarm. Add the warm milk to the yogurt starter gradually, mixing well. Pour the mixture into jars, and cover the tops of the jars with a light cloth or towel. Put the jars in a warm place, such as an unlit oven or next to a hot water pipe, for 4 to 6 hours, or until the mixture has thickened. Put lids on the jars and store your homemade yogurt in the refrigerator.

Note: Remember to save some of the yogurt to use as starter.

Cutting the High Cost of Meat

With a sharp knife and a sharp eye for bargains, you can save as much as 50 percent on your meat bill, if you're willing to do some of the butcher's work yourself. Any time a piece of meat is cut and trimmed for your convenience and arranged prettily with a sprig of parsley at the supermarket, it's going to cost you more than it should. We are especially wary of those large, flat packages in which meat pieces are laid out like jewels on a velvet tray. You often see beef kabobs, very thin rib-eye steaks, and steaks cut from the eye of the round roast packaged this way, and, sometimes, chicken drumsticks, too. The large, flat package is an optical illusion designed to make you think you're getting a lot. Don't be fooled. Look at the actual meat weight, and don't pay for that pretty packaging! Instead, find the larger pieces of meat from which these cuts originated, cut them up at home, and lay them out beautifully on a platter after you've cooked them.

Chicken

A whole chicken is cheaper than its parts. That's rule one! If you buy legs and thighs in one package, breasts in another, and wings in yet another, you can be sure you're paying more per pound than you would for the whole chicken. It doesn't take long to learn to cut up a chicken yourself. Just study the structure, and feel for the bones and joints. It's worth the effort in the savings you realize.

If you have an adequate freezer, we suggest you buy several (four, at least) chickens when they are on sale. Wash them in cold water (always), drain, and cut them up before freezing. Then you, too, can package drumsticks in one bag, wings in another, and save chicken breasts for that special recipe. Or wrap together a variety of pieces in meal-size portions. Collect the backs, necks, and giblets to make stock or to cook for your pets. Freeze the livers until you get enough together to really do something with them. How you package your home-cut chicken pieces depends, of course, on how you expect to use them.

Turkey

Do you buy turkey parts because a big turkey is too much to eat at one time? Why not buy the whole turkey anyway, which will be cheaper per pound, and cut it up into parts? Just think of it as a large chicken. Freeze the parts separately, and you'll have all kinds of turkey dinners waiting for you without the worry about endless leftovers.

Veal

We love veal cutlets, but we don't love the current price—nor do we pay it. Instead, we buy veal leg when it's on sale and remove the larger muscle. (A piece of meat with no separations in it is called a muscle. The white tissue surrounding it is sinew or fat.) Freeze this muscle until it is stiff but not solidly frozen; keep testing it so that it won't become impossible to cut. When it's ready, you'll be able to slice nice thin cutlets from this piece of veal. Lay them out with plastic wrap between each layer and freeze them in meal-size packages.

The rest of the veal leg can be cut up for stew or cacciatore. The leg bone is prized for stock, but we often use it to flavor a tomato sauce.

Lamb

Shish kabobs of lamb are cut from the shoulder or leg. If you do the cutting yourself, it will be a lot cheaper than the ready-cut ones in the meat case. Compare prices, taking the bone into consideration. Remember, too, that the bone makes a nice Scotch broth!

Beef

Round steak is not really tender steak, but it's a good buy because there's little waste. To get the most, and the best, out of a round steak, buy the full cut and divide it (see figure) into (A) top round, tender enough to broil or pan-broil; (B) bottom round, which needs moist cooking or braising; and (C) eye of the round, not as tender as top round, but okay to slice thin for Oriental dishes (slice when partially frozen). If your family is large, buy more than one round steak so that each division will be enough for one meal.

Blade chuck roast or steak is frequently on sale, perhaps because it's just another pot roast if you leave it in one piece. However, if you choose the blade chuck roast with a bone in it that really looks like a knife blade and not a T, you can get nice tender steak out of part of it. The roast with the blade bone is the

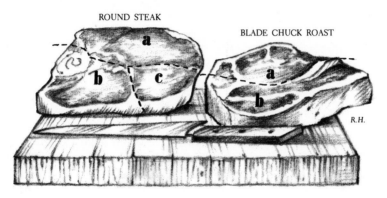

ROUND STEAK

BLADE CHUCK ROAST

R.H.

"first cut," meaning it came off the beef carcass from the side nearest the rib roast. The rib-eye (the same rib-eye for which you pay a premium if it's marked rib-eye steak) extends into this particular blade chuck roast. Divide the roast (see figure) into (A) the rib portion, and (B) the stewing portion. Broil or pan-broil A. Cut up B for braised beef. Save the bone to make stock. We have carefully done this and weighed the results, minus waste, pricing each piece according to its current market value, and find we save 50 percent. Again, it pays to buy more than one blade chuck roast and to cut them at the same time, if you have the freezer space.

There's a trick to buying a good sirloin steak, too. For maximum tenderness, buy the one with the long flat bone or pin bone rather than the round bone. If top and bottom sirloin are sold separately, the top sirloin is the better of the two.

Butchers sometimes slice pieces from the eye of the round roast to sell as minute steaks. It's cheaper to do this slicing yourself, and, if you're going to do that much, you might as well buy the cheaper rump roast instead and cut your sandwich steaks from that.

Pork

The blade-end pork roast is usually an outstanding buy. You can roast it "as is," or bone it (save the bone for making a tomato sauce). You can cut the roast into chops. Or you can cut off all the meat and fat and grind them into sausage with the addition of some spices. Form the sausage into patties, and freeze them until needed. There are no preservatives in homemade sausages! Here's the basic recipe:

Basic Pork Sausage

1 pound ground pork and pork fat	$^{1}/_{2}$ teaspoon black pepper
1 teaspoon salt	2 teaspoons sage

Mix all ingredients, form into patties, and freeze until needed. *Yield:* 1 pound.

Garlic Sausage

Make Basic Pork Sausage, and add 1 finely minced clove of garlic.

Italian Sausage

Make Basic Pork Sausage, adding $^{1}/_{2}$ teaspoon fennel seeds and 2 teaspoons paprika.

Country Sausage

Make Basic Pork Sausage, adding $^{1}/_{4}$ teaspoon ground thyme and $^{1}/_{2}$ teaspoon ground marjoram.

Spiced Sausage

Make Basic Pork Sausage, adding $^{1}/_{4}$ teaspoon ground cloves and $^{1}/_{4}$ teaspoon ground mace.

TENDERIZERS

The tannin in tea and papain in papaya fruit are both natural meat tenderizers. (Papain is the chief ingredient in commercial meat tenderizers.) If you live in an area where ripe papayas are available, surround an oven-braised beef with slices of the fruit while it cooks; this will make it more tender. Fortunately, tea is available everywhere, so, in lieu of papaya, use strong tea as part of the liquid in a pot roast or stew that may be tough. For flavor, use double strength beef stock for the rest of the liquid (about half tea and half stock).

Fun Foods

Almost every family has its nibblers—the ones who are perpetually rummaging through the kitchen cupboards or the refrigerator searching for something to eat or drink. Keeping these snackers satisfied by buying the array of foods offered in the supermarkets can put your family budget in the red and keep it there. A partial solution is to keep a supply of fresh fruits and nuts on hand. The ardent snackers, however, are only temporarily put off with treats of this type. They want the "real thing"—the sticky candy, the crunchy potato chips, the sweet drinks. Our solution is to make these foods ourselves. It saves money and it eliminates the potential hazards of a steady diet of sugar-laden, additive-ridden food. While we do use some sugar, we don't overuse it, and, of course, our snacks don't contain as many preservatives as their commercial counterparts do. They're fun foods instead of junk foods. We have fun making them, and our families seem happy with the results.

BEVERAGES

One thing that keeps the refrigerator door opening and closing constantly in most homes is what seems to be unquenchable thirst. Especially in summer, when the thermometer climbs and children are out of school, the shout heard 'round most kitchens is, "What do you have to drink?" These are some of our favorite answers to that question.

Mock Champagne

Served in champagne glasses, this drink is a delicious substitute for the real thing and lets children join in the festivities when adults are toasting a special occasion.

> 3 cups apple juice
> 2 cups soda water or quinine water

Mix together and chill. (Or chill the ingredients separately and mix individual "cocktails" in a ratio of 3 parts apple juice to two parts soda.) *Yield:* 5 cups.

Mello-Orange Blend

> 1 cantaloupe, peeled, seeded, and   1/4 cup lime juice
>   cut into small pieces   1 tablespoon sugar
> 1 cup fresh orange juice   1 cup cold water

Blend all the ingredients well in the blender. If your blender container is a small one, blend in two batches. Chill. *Yield:* 4 servings.

Rhubarb Cocktail (Nova Scotia Special)

3 pounds rhubarb
2 1/2 quarts water
2 cups sugar

1/2 teaspoon cinnamon
2 cups unsweetened orange juice
2 teaspoons lemon juice

Wash the rhubarb and cut it into pieces about 2 inches long. In a large saucepan, simmer the rhubarb in water, covered, until it's very soft. Remove from heat and strain the juice into a container. Discard rhubarb pulp. Add the sugar and cinnamon to the juice and stir until the sugar is dissolved. Cool; add orange juice and lemon juice, and chill before serving. *Yield:* about 2 quarts.

Fresh Tomato Juice

Caution: This is so much tastier than the canned variety that, once your family has sampled it, you'll never get away with serving commercial tomato juice again.

18 large, ripe tomatoes
3/4 cup water
1 teaspoon celery salt

1 small onion, peeled
1/2 teaspoon sugar
1 tablespoon lemon juice

Core and cut up the tomatoes. Place all ingredients in a large pan, and bring to a boil over medium-high heat. Reduce heat and simmer for 1/2 hour. Remove and discard the onion, and strain the remaining ingredients. Bottle the juice and keep in refrigerator. *Yield:* 6 servings.

Note: Because this fresh juice isn't homogenized, it may separate. Shake it well before serving.

Super Milk Shake

This drink and the one below are delicious, nutritious, and serve as good quick lunches on busy days or as after-school or bedtime snacks. Even reluctant milk drinkers go for them.

1 ripe banana
1 egg, slightly beaten
1 cup milk

1 1/2 teaspoons sugar
1/2 teaspoon vanilla extract

Slice bananas into a blender container; blend. Add the egg and a little of the milk; blend until the egg and banana are well mixed. Add the remaining ingredients and blend again. *Yield:* 1 large shake.

Nutrition Nog

1 cup milk
1 tablespoon molasses
1 egg

1/4 teaspoon vanilla extract
1 teaspoon brewer's yeast

Put all ingredients in a blender container and blend thoroughly. If the drink isn't sweet enough, add honey to taste and blend again. *Yield:* 1 serving.

Good-Tasting Instant Milk

If your budget says "instant milk," and your family says "no!" try this:

1 quart prepared nonfat dry milk
1/2 teaspoon vanilla extract
1 1/2 teaspoons sugar or honey to taste

Mix all ingredients well and chill. *Yield:* 1 quart.

SNACKS

Potato Chips

Parties and potato chips just seem to go together—and making your own potato chips is fun! It's challenging too, and guests never fail to be impressed with the host or hostess who serves homemade chips. Last, but by no means least, they really do taste better than the commercial kind and they cost about one-third as much to make. (Use potatoes with smooth, unblemished skins, and be sure that they haven't sprouted.

> 12 small or 9 medium-sized potatoes
> oil for frying (either corn or peanut oil works well)
> salt to taste

Peel the potatoes and slice them very thin, using a vegetable cutter or potato peeler. As you slice them, place each slice in a bowl half-full of ice-cold water. When all are sliced, place the bowl in the refrigerator for about 1^1/$_2$ hours.

Fill a deep fryer (a deep saucepan and frying basket can be substituted) half-full of oil, and heat the oil to 350°F (175°C). While the oil is heating, dry the potato slices on paper towels. Deep fry them, a few at a time, until they are lightly browned. Try to maintain the frying temperature of 350°F (175°C). Drain the potato chips and pat off the excess oil with paper towels. Salt to taste, and let cool before serving. *Yield:* 12 portions.

Easy Peanut Clusters

These disappear almost as fast as we can make them!

> 2 cups chocolate bits
> 3 tablespoons peanut butter
> 4 cups chopped peanuts

In the top of a double boiler over medium heat, melt the chocolate and peanut butter together. Stir until the mixture is smooth. Put the peanuts in a large heated bowl (warm it with hot water or in a warm oven) and mix in the melted chocolate. Drop by spoonfuls onto a greased cookie sheet. Refrigerate. *Yield:* about 3 dozen pieces.

Note: You may substitute 1 cup of raisins for 1 cup of the peanuts.

Caramel Apples

There's no resistance to an apple a day when it's presented this way!

> 6 red apples
> 6 lollipop sticks
> 1 pound caramels
>
> ^{1}/$_4$ cup water
> ^{1}/$_2$ cup finely ground nuts

Remove the stems from the apples. Wash and dry them and insert lollipop sticks in the stem ends. In the top of a double boiler over boiling water, melt the caramels in ^{1}/$_4$ cup water, stirring constantly. When the caramel mixture is smooth, dip the apples in it one by one, tipping the pan to coat the entire apple. Roll the caramel apples in the nuts and put them on a greased cookie sheet. Refrigerate until the caramel has hardened.

Popcorn Balls

6 cups popcorn, popped according to package directions	2 cups brown sugar
	8 tablespoons water
2 cups unsalted peanuts	1/2 teaspoon vanilla extract
2 tablespoons butter	

In a medium-sized saucepan, melt the butter; add brown sugar and water. Bring to the boiling point over medium heat, stirring constantly. Cover the pan, reduce heat, and cook for 5 minutes. Remove cover and continue cooking until syrup reaches about 235°F (113°C) on a candy thermometer or a bit of the syrup dropped from the spoon forms a soft ball which flattens out when you pick it up.

Put the popcorn in a large bowl and pour the syrup over it, mixing well to coat all of the popcorn. Cool the mixture just long enough so that you can handle it comfortably. Oil your hands, and roll the popcorn into balls. *Yield:* about 30 balls.

Old-Time American Doughnuts

1 cup milk	1/2 teaspoon nutmeg
1 tablespoon lemon juice	2 eggs
3 1/2 cups sifted all-purpose flour	1 cup sugar
4 teaspoons baking powder	2 tablespoons melted butter, cooled
1 teaspoon baking soda	fat for deep frying
1/2 teaspoon salt	

Add the lemon juice to the milk and set aside. Sift the dry ingredients (except sugar) together. Beat the eggs and sugar together until well blended and light; stir in the melted butter. Now add the dry ingredients alternately with the milk to the egg-sugar mixture. Do not overbeat.

Chill the dough for at least an hour to make it easier to handle. On a lightly floured surface, roll out the dough so it's 1/4 inch thick. Cut with a doughnut cutter. Heat fat to 375°F (190°C). Fry the doughnuts a few at a time until they are golden brown on both sides. Do not prick them with a fork, but turn with a spoon instead. Try to maintain an even frying temperature. Drain on absorbent paper and sprinkle with cinnamon-sugar, if desired. Serve hot. *Yield:* 3 dozen.

Baby Foods:
Love and a Well-Balanced Diet

The giant baby-food industry is growing rich by cooking large vats of foods, pureeing or chopping them, sealing them in tiny jars, and selling them as baby foods. Why not prepare these baby foods at home? It's easy and it saves money.

A baby doesn't need an infinite variety of foods. He needs only a balanced representation from each of the basic four food groups (grains, milk, fruits and vegetables, and meat), just as an adult does. Of course, baby starts off subsisting on milk, but usually by the time he's reached the age of six months, he has been introduced to foods from all of the groups. You should consult with baby's pediatrician to establish when any certain food should be started. *Always* check with him before giving your baby a food he hasn't had before.

Many of the meals you serve your family can also be served to your baby. Set his portion aside before you use seasoning. When you're ready to prepare the baby food, add liquid and blend it with the food in your blender. As your baby grows, you can decrease the blending time and the amount of liquid, so that foods go gradually from a very fine puree to a chopped consistency.

If you find something you've prepared is too thick, thin it down a bit with orange juice, pineapple juice, tomato juice, or the water in which you've cooked a mild vegetable. To thicken food that has become overblended or too watery, add a little nonfat dry milk or finely grated egg yolk.

Is it really cheaper to make your baby's food? Indeed it is! If you serve him from the meals you prepare for the rest of the family, the additional cost of the portion is almost negligible. For instance, the egg yolk that can be purchased in those expensive little jars (the jars themselves account for about a third of the cost of commercial baby foods) costs about two-and-a-half times as much as the fresh, hard-boiled egg yolk you can prepare at home. Home-prepared meats, fruits, and vegetables for baby cost about half as much as those in the stores; and with most juices, you have a whopping two-thirds savings when you choose home-prepared.

If you're convinced that homemade is the way to go, there are a few simple things you should know about preparing baby foods at home. First, you should have a good blender—it's your main tool.

Second, when preparing foods for your baby, never add salt or sugar. The salt you feed your baby now may contribute to high-blood pressure later in life. All the salt that the body needs occurs naturally in foods. Sugar is also of questionable food value for people of any age. Why take chances with your baby's health? If a food needs sweetening, use honey (which is far easier to digest than sugar) or molasses (which will add iron to your child's diet). Sugar also occurs naturally in a great many foods, such as fruits and vegetables, so don't worry that your baby will be lacking either salt or sugar.

Third, storing homemade baby foods is as easy as making them. Pureed foods keep in the refrigerator for one or two days. To keep them longer, put them in ice cube trays and freeze them solidly. Of course, you will need the ice cube trays for other uses, so empty the contents, wrap each cube in plastic wrap, and store the cubes in a labeled plastic bag or container. At a temperature of 0°F (−18°C) or less, you can keep homemade baby food for months in the freezer. When you defrost them later, do so in the refrigerator or right in the warming pan. Don't leave them to defrost at room temperature. Frozen foods always taste best if they are simmered a bit and then served at a comfortable warm temperature. *Note:* Potatoes and custard mixtures don't freeze well.

Fourth, naturally, you need to use super-clean utensils when preparing any foods for your infant. We also recommend that you cook in stainless steel or glass pans—there is some question about the health risks involved in using aluminum and Teflon.

Here are ways to prepare baby foods at home, as well as some of our favorite recipes:

Cereal

Cereal is usually baby's first food. You can use many of the cereals you buy for the rest of your family. Oatmeal, for instance, need only be ground to a finer consistency by blending it in your blender before cooking it. A puree of rice and barley is a pleasant change that will fill baby's daily need for a grain product. When you purchase rice, however, be sure the label says "enriched." This means that some of the vitamins and minerals lost in processing have been replaced.

Fruits

Bake fruits in a very small amount of water in a covered dish until the fruit is soft. The time varies depending on the fruit—an apple takes about an hour to bake. After the fruit is cooked, peel it, remove the seeds or core (if you haven't done so before cooking), and place the pulp along with the cooking juice into the blender container. Blend to the desired consistency. Young baby's digestive system can't handle raw fruit, but, as your baby grows older, you will be able to eliminate the cooking step in preparing soft fruits. Your pediatrician can advise you when your baby can begin to enjoy the superior nutritive benefits of eating raw fruit. One exception to the "no raw fruit" rule is the banana. At an early age, baby can eat ripe raw bananas. They are very digestible mashed with a bit of milk.

Juices

Either fresh or frozen juices can be given to babies. Dilute to the strength suggested by your pediatrician, and then strain the juice through clean cheesecloth so that it will flow freely through a nipple.

Vegetables

Whether you're using fresh or frozen vegetables, the best method of cooking them for maximum nutritional value is steaming. A steaming basket that is adjustable and will fit inside almost any pan is an inexpensive addition to your kitchen equipment. Put a small amount of water in the bottom of the pan, add the steaming basket with the vegetable in it, cover the pan tightly, and bring the water to a boil. The length of time you allow for steaming depends on the vegetables, but cook until the vegetable is soft. Puree it in your blender, adding just enough cooking water to attain the consistency your baby needs.

Meat

To prepare meat for your baby, blend one-half cup of cooked, cubed, unseasoned meat (right from the family meal) with 5 tablespoons of liquid. Use either the water you have cooked vegetables in or a compatible juice, such as apple juice with pork, orange juice with chicken, or tomato juice with beef. If you wish, you can add a few tablespoons of cooked vegetable and blend it right in with the meat. What could be easier!

Eggs

The first egg that a baby should have is the hard-boiled yolk mashed up with a little milk. Later, scrambled eggs, lightly cooked in a little vegetable oil, can be added to the diet. Egg custard is a dessert that babies love, and it's so good for them!

Yogurt

Yogurt is an ideal food for everyone, and baby's no exception. You can blend yogurt (for homemade, see page 87–88) with either vegetables or fruits. It aids digestion, and may turn a fussy baby with a stomachache into a happy baby.

The following recipes are a few food combinations we think your baby might enjoy. By all means, experiment with combinations of your own, but bear in mind the four basic food groups and your child's need for a well-balanced diet.

Chicken Hawaiian Puree

3/4 cup juice from canned pineapple
1 cup cubed chicken, cooked
1/2 cup canned pineapple, crushed
1/2 cup cooked rice

Put the pineapple juice in the blender container. Add the chicken and blend. Add the crushed pineapple and rice, and blend until the mixture is pureed. Freeze in an ice cube tray. *Yield:* about 1 ice cube tray.

Peachy-Pear Puree

1/2 pound peaches
1/2 pound pears
3 tablespoons water

Preheat oven to 350°F (175°C). Wash the fruit and core the pears. Bake them with the water in a covered baking dish in a preheated oven for 25 minutes, or until the fruit is soft. Remove the dish from the oven and let the fruit stand until cool. Peel, or scrape the pulp from the pears. Peel and remove the pits from the peaches. Blend the fruits together until they are pureed. Freeze in an ice cube tray. *Yield:* about 1 ice cube tray.

Apple, Orange, Banana Delight

1 apple, large (McIntosh is a good choice)
1 seedless orange, large
1 banana, ripe

Wash, peel, core and cut the apple into chunks. Peel and section the orange. Peel and slice the banana. Put all the fruit in a blender and puree (if more liquid is needed, use orange juice). Freeze in ice cube tray. *Yield:* about 1/2 an ice cube tray.

Note: Since this is not cooked, it's not a first-time fruit, but is meant for a baby about six months or older.

Liver and Onions

1 cup broiled baby beef liver, chopped
3/4 cup cooked pulp of acorn or butternut squash
1 teaspoon boiled, chopped onion
1/2 cup egg noodles, cooked
3/4 cup water

Blend all the ingredients together and you have a complete dinner for your baby. Freeze in an ice cube tray. *Yield:* about 1 ice cube tray.

Carrot Juice

This is an aid in times of infant diarrhea.

1 medium-sized carrot
1 cup skim milk

Wash and scrape the carrot well. Cut off the ends and slice the carrot into a blender container. Add the milk and blend thoroughly. Strain and use at once. *Yield:* 8 ounces.

1 cup tomato juice, unseasoned $^2/_3$ cup cooked sliced carrots
1 cup cooked, cubed beef $^2/_3$ cup cooked macaroni

Put the tomato juice in a blender container. Add the beef cubes and puree. Add the carrots and macaroni and blend to desired consistency. Freeze in ice cube tray. *Yield:* about 1 ice cube tray (probably a bit more).

Pet Foods:
Square Meals for Dogs and Cats

There are at least three good reasons why you might want to make your own pet food—to feed your dog or cat more nutritiously, to save money, and to "spoil" your pet more intelligently. The most important factor in animal health is a balanced diet proper to that species. And, as in everything else, homemade tastes best. Your pet will demonstrate appreciation in his own wordless fashion!

NUTRITION

The *minimum* protein requirement for dogs is 5.5 percent of their total intake, according to the National Research Council, but this applies only to healthy adult dogs. In times of stress, illness, or even extremes of weather—in fact, to meet all the vicissitudes and stages of life—20 to 25 percent protein is recommended. Cats need 50 percent more protein than dogs and are known to be rather fussy about how they get it.

Protein, however, does not supply all of a pet's nutritional needs, and, indeed, a dog or cat fed only protein foods will eventually suffer from malnutrition.

Grain foods and vegetables are the natural supplements to meat and fish and should be included regularly in your pet's diet. Grains supply needed carbohydrates as well as many vitamins, and they assist the protein to work properly. Vegetables add roughage along with their high vitamin and mineral content, thus assuring proper digestion. Wild animals solve this problem by eating the whole carcass of their prey, including the stomach which often contains grains, seeds, and plant materials.

Furry animals require a higher percentage of fat in their meals than humans do—7 percent for dogs, and more for cats—to maintain glossy coats and healthy skin. Not enough fat leads to an excess of dander ("dandruff" in humans), to which many people are allergic. This does not mean you should feed your pet unlimited meat fat. For a dander problem, a tablespoon or two of salad oil per day is recommended, depending, of course, on the size and weight of the animal (a teaspoon for the little ones!). Vegetable oil in a cat's diet helps to deal with swallowed hair.

In addition, your pet needs almost as many vitamins and minerals as you do *on a daily basis*, since only vitamins A and D can be stored in the body for any length of time. A well-balanced and varied diet should provide for their nutritional needs. The most important dietary supplements to give to puppies (who use them up fast in their growing process) are cod liver oil (vitamins A and D) and calcium. The calcium intake for puppies should be monitored, considering all sources. The right amount builds strong bones and teeth; too much can cause lameness in the larger breeds. Healthy adult dogs require no supplements if they are given a well-balanced diet. Give vitamin A to both kittens and cats as a preventive to urinary gravel and stones.

Animals need water, too, preferably available at all times. Cats are sometimes loathe to drink the water they need (about eight ounces per day) even though they are prone to kidney and bladder disorders. There should always be sufficient moisture in their food to take the place of the water they won't drink. Homemade soup for cats can help make up for this deficiency.

Eggs and milk are fine foods for pets, with some reservations. Eggs must always be cooked, because uncooked egg white destroys biotin, an essential vitamin, in the intestines. Dry milk is better than whole milk because whole milk can cause diarrhea in adult dogs. When preparing food for puppies, however, whole milk is used and even enriched with cream and/or egg yolk in order to better match their mother's milk, which is richer than cow's milk. Other dairy products, such as cottage cheese and pot cheese, can be given pets, and they are generally relished by them.

There are three kinds of pet food on the market—dry grain food or kibble, canned food, and the burger-patty type (canned food without the can). Owners of large breeds of dogs sometimes choose kibble because it is nutritionally balanced and cheap. The problem is that it is the least flavorful, and the animal may not eat enough of it to supply his daily needs.

To counter the taste problem of kibble, many owners combine kibble with canned food, or use canned food alone if the animal is a small one. Some canned foods are all meat and some are a mixture of meat and grain, the all-meat kind being the most expensive. Water makes up a large part of the weight of canned pet foods. It takes four cans to equal the bulk of two cups of dry food.

If you read the labels of canned foods carefully, you will probably notice that *meat by-products* are frequently listed before *meat*, meaning the percentage of by-products is greater. The FDA reports that the meat and meat by-products contained in canned foods are often "derived from animals that have died other than by slaughter. . . . Because of high cooking temperatures, the products should not pose a health problem." Still, you may prefer that your pet be fed on meat from animals that have not perished from old age.

The burger-patty type of pet food also has a high moisture content (25 percent). The flavor is generally attractive to animals. To maintain product stability and prevent spoilage, a number of non-food preservatives are required. For the same reason, many of these burgers contain a large proportion of sugar, which retards the growth of bacteria. Sugar is not good for animals, and, in some individual pets, can prove indigestible, resulting in diarrhea or vomiting.

Before leaving the subject of nutrition, we'd like to dispel a couple of myths. Dogs *can* digest starchy vegetables, although they are not recommended for cats. Raw meat does *not* make an animal vicious. In fact, some experts recommend that cats have one raw meat meal a day.

COST

According to statisticians, Americans spend $2 billion a year on pet foods, which even outsell baby foods. The prospects of increasing profits stimulate manufacturers to create a variety of new products, many of which hike your food bill needlessly.

If you are in the habit of feeding your pet reward foods and treats such as flavored crackers or bone-shaped biscuits, you can realize about a 75 percent saving by making these yourself at home. Since you will not be adding preservatives, if you make a large batch it is wise to freeze anything more than a few days' supply.

Speaking of treats, there's no treat a dog likes better than a delicious beef marrow bone, which is the only kind we feel is sturdy enough for our dogs. Puppies can benefit by using bones to cut their teeth, and older dogs clean the tartar from their teeth while chewing on a favorite bone. Once they're well cleaned off, we boil the bones to remove any traces of grease and keep them around the house for a rainy day. Beef marrow bones cost only a few cents, but the joy of them lives on and on, unlike rawhide chews that a larger breed of dog can demolish in an afternoon.

Making your own meat or fish food to give cats and small dogs or to mix with kibble for the big eaters will save 20 percent or more, depending on your shopping skill.

Some dog owners never think of fish as a pet food, which is a shame, because it is highly nutritious and dogs love it, the fishier the better. This is a special economy bonus for a family with a fisherman who brings home a large catch. Cats, on the other hand, are generally fed too much fish for their delicate digestions. Some animal nutritionists say that one fish meal per week is about the right amount for our feline friends. All bones, large or small, must be removed from fish for animals. After all the obvious ones have been taken out, you can, if you wish, grind the fish in the blender instead of removing all the small ones. Although it may sound strange to you, your pet will probably not object to a mixture (freshly combined) of fish and meat. Think of it as a Surf 'n Turf dinner!

In giving dogs organ meats, use only a tablespoon or two, since too much can cause diarrhea. They are so inexpensive (especially when on sale) and so nutritious that it is worth the effort to find out just how much your individual pet's digestion will tolerate. In fact, whenever you introduce a new food to your pet, start with a very small amount, just as you would in feeding an unfamiliar food to a child. Pets can have food allergies, too!

There's no way you can make kibble for less than you can buy it, so we recommend using that to provide sufficient bulk for your St. Bernard or German Shepherd. The better brands have a dependable balanced nutrition. Your homemade meat or fish "mixer" combined with this dry food will provide the flavor that keeps your large dog eating eagerly. Moistening dry food insures that it will swell in the dish rather than in his stomach.

Dry milk is the cheapest form of milk and the best for adult pets.

"SPOILING" YOUR PETS INTELLIGENTLY

Animals, being color blind, choose their foods by smell. Although individual tastes vary, most dogs love gamey flavors best and enjoy the taste of liver, fat, lamb, horsemeat, beef, cheese, fish, garlic, and onion. Cats relish chicken, turkey, lamb, liver, fish, and yeast, and prefer fresh to aged flavors. Animals do not require salt to make their food tasty. The natural salt found *in* foods is sufficient for them.

Cats being the fussy eaters of the pet world, it is not wise to continually feed them their favorite foods to the exclusion of others. Soon they will refuse to eat a balanced ration. Instead, reserve these favorites to mix with and spark up the less desired foods they need, like grains.

Catnip is a special treat that cats groove on, and, needless to say, you can grow your own for maximum economy, if you can find a place to hide the plant from your cat. Only the leaves should be given, not the stems. A cat who has catnip regularly is less liable to go wild over it than one who gets only a little catnip once in a while. Catnip is an aphrodisiac, however, and one ought not to give it to unaltered animals.

Cats should be fed three times a day, and the food finely ground. A blender does this job easily. Adults dogs need only one meal a day, but people who spoil their dogs may want to give them a bit of breakfast, too. This prevents them from gobbling too fast at dinnertime.

Ground beef for cats should be lean, but the amount they eat is very small. Economy-grade ground beef is all right for dogs, if you cook it and pour off the fat. Spiced meats, ham, pork, raw fish, salt fish, raw poultry, sweets, or alcoholic beverages should *not* be fed to animals. Cooked oatmeal, cornmeal, rice, whole wheat bread, and wheat germ can be added to pet food, and they are wise additions to meat meals.

Dogs may eat any vegetables they want, but cats should not have the starchy ones, like peas and corn. A little experimentation will soon reveal which ones your pet prefers. Some pets will enjoy certain fruits. One dog we know will eat yellow apples but not red ones. It's all right for a pet to have a taste of melon or seedless grape or whatever he fancies now and then. Many pets, however, think of fruit as a weird human habit and would much prefer a bit of raw meat.

Once you get into the habit of making your own pet food, you'll find that it's really just a little trouble to give a great deal of pleasure and save money, too!

R.H.

The following recipes give their yield in amount or weight, but, of course, it's up to you to decide how much is proper for your animal's size and whether or not kibble is to be added. It is always advisable to add some kibble or grain food such as wheat germ, cooked oatmeal, or whole wheat bread to any meat dinner. For dogs, a good proportion would be 75 percent carbohydrate foods (grain and vegetables) to 25 percent meat; for cats, half carbohydrate foods and half meat. Cats are usually given 3 ounces or less per meal. A 30-pound dog will eat about $10^{1}/_{2}$ ounces of food; a 60-pound dog is usually given a pound or more per day. But these figures are very general and should be adapted to the specific needs and condition of your pet. Nursing mothers, for example, might eat twice their normal amount, and dry milk would be included in their diets.

Remember that all pet foods should be served warm or at room temperature, not freezing cold from the refrigerator nor boiling hot from the stove.

Sloppy Joes (for dogs)

$^{1}/_{4}$ pound ground beef (economy grade)
dash of garlic powder (optional)

In a medium-sized skillet, fry the ground beef until lightly browned; add garlic powder. Drain off all the fat. Use the beef as a mixer with kibble, and add water to moisten the mixture. *Yield:* about 1 cup.

Note: Economy-grade beef can sometimes be purchased very inexpensively in four-pound packages on sale. We buy it this way and freeze it in the amount we will cook for one meal for our dogs. If you forget to defrost it ahead of time, it can be cooked frozen with the addition of a cover to the pan. Break up the meat from time to time as it defrosts in the pan.

Steak Tartare (for cats)

2 ounces lean ground beef
2 ounces beef broth

Put the raw beef in a small saucepan and warm it just enough to take off the refrigerator chill but not enough to cook it. Warm the beef broth, and combine the two. *Yield:* 4 ounces.

Mackerel Dinner (for dogs and cats)

1 small mackerel
1 teaspoon corn oil
$^{1}/_{2}$ cup water

In a skillet, heat the oil and fry the mackerel until it is cooked through and flakes apart easily with a fork. Remove fish from the pan and allow it to cool. Pour the water into the hot pan and scrape into it all the brown bits. Reserve. Remove all bones from the fish. *For dogs:* Separate the fish into flakes with your fingers. Use with pan juices as a mixer in kibble. *For cats:* Grind the fish in a blender, using the pan juices to moisten. *Yield:* about 2 cups.

Sautéed Liver (for dogs and cats)

1 slice beef liver (about $^{1}/_{4}$ pound)
1 teaspoon corn oil
$^{1}/_{2}$ cup water

Heat oil in a skillet. Add the beef liver and fry on both sides until cooked through but not dry inside. Remove the liver from the pan. Add the water to the pan and scrape into it all the brown bits. Reserve. *For dogs:* Cut the liver into pieces. Use about half (or as much as you know will agree with your pet) as a mixer with the pan juices. Save the rest for another meal. *For cats:* Grind the liver in a blender, using the pan juices to moisten. Use as a mixer with other foods. Freeze extra in serving-size portions. *Yield:* about 1 cup diced, 1½ cups ground liver.

Note: The best buy in liver is beef liver, frozen, when it is on sale.

Veal Stew (for dogs and cats)

½ pound stewing veal (the inexpensive kind with bones)	1 chicken bouillon cube
	½ onion, chopped
1 cup canned tomatoes, with juice	1 tablespoon chopped fresh parsley
1 cup water	dash of garlic powder

Combine all ingredients in a pot and simmer, covered, until the meat is tender (about 1 hour), or cook 15 minutes in a pressure cooker. Remove all the bones. *For dogs:* Chop the meat and return it to the stew. Use as a mixer with kibble. *For cats:* Grind the stew in a blender. Add a teaspoon of wheat germ or a half slice of whole wheat bread. Freeze the extra in serving-size portions. *Yield:* about 3 cups.

Note: This dish smells so delicious during cooking that you will have to guard it carefully lest it be consumed by a family member.

Lamb Stew (for dogs and cats)

Substitute lamb chunks for the veal in the preceding recipe. Omit tomato, if desired.

Chicken Soup (for dogs and cats)

This recipe answers the question of what to do with that chicken liver, heart, and other goodies left from the purchase of a whole chicken.

1 chicken liver	1 chicken neck
1 giblet	2 cups water
1 chicken heart	1 tablespoon chopped fresh parsley

Combine all ingredients in a saucepan. Cover and simmer until the giblet is tender (about 1 hour). *For dogs:* Chop the liver, giblet, heart, chicken neck skin, and as much of the meat from the neck as you have the patience to take off. Be certain there are no bones left in the meat. Return the meat to the soup. Use as a mixer with kibble. *For cats:* Prepare the meat as for dogs. Grind the meat in a blender with sufficient broth to moisten. *Yield:* about 2½ cups.

Beef Kidney Soup (for dogs)

1 medium-size beef kidney, trimmed of fat	1 carrot, sliced
	½ onion, chopped
3 cups water	dash of garlic powder

Combine all ingredients in a pot and simmer until tender (about 1 hour), or cook 15 minutes in a pressure cooker. Chop the beef kidney and return it to the soup. Use sparingly as a mixer with kibble. The extra may be frozen in serving-size portions. *Yield:* 1 quart.

Beef Kidney Soup (for cats)

1 medium-size beef kidney, trimmed of fat
2 cups water
1/2 onion, chopped

Simmer all ingredients in a pot until tender (about 1 hour), or cook 15 minutes in a pressure cooker. Grind all ingredients in a blender, and use as a mixer with other foods. Freeze the extra in serving-size portions. *Yield:* 3 to 3 1/2 cups.

Invalid's Delight (for dogs)

2/3 pound ground beef
water to cover
3 cups cooked rice

In a saucepan, combine the ground beef with water to cover. Boil 5 minutes, and drain thoroughly. Mix with cooked rice. *Yield:* about 4 cups.

Note: This dish is recommended for dogs recovering from a digestive upset, such as diarrhea. Do *not* mix with kibble or vegetables.

Heavily sugared foods aren't good for animals, and they would much rather have their treats flavored with liver, cheese, wheat, fish, and other delectable tastes anyway. The price of commercial pet treats is surprisingly high compared to the following recipes which you can make at home for a few minutes time and a few cents.

Liver Cookies

1/2 cup dry milk
1/2 cup (approximately) wheat germ
1 teaspoon honey
1 3 1/2-ounce jar strained baby food

liver, or the same amount made at home in the blender with cooked liver and broth to moisten

Preheat oven to 350°F (175°C). Combine the milk powder and wheat germ; drizzle honey on top. Add the liver, stirring until everything is well mixed. If it is too soft to handle, add more wheat germ. Form the mixture into balls. Place them on an oiled cookie sheet, and flatten them slightly with a fork. Bake 8 to 10 minutes. The bottoms should be brown but not burned. Consistency will be fudgy. Store them in a closed glass jar in the refrigerator. Freeze anything more than a few days' supply. *Yield:* 20 cookies.

Beef Cookies

Follow the preceding recipe, substituting for the liver a 3 1/2-ounce jar strained baby food beef or the homemade equivalent.

Fish Cookies

Follow the recipe for Liver Cookies, using 3 1/2 ounces of finely mashed, canned boned mackerel or freshly cooked boned mackerel instead of the liver.

Wheaty Biscuits

3 cups white all-purpose flour
3 cups whole wheat flour
$^1/_2$ cup wheat germ
1 cup cornmeal
1 cup uncooked oatmeal

$^1/_2$ cup dry milk
$^1/_4$ cup honey
$6^1/_4$ cups (approximately) chicken or
    beef stock or prepared bouillon
1 egg mixed with 2 tablespoons milk

Preheat oven to 300°F (150°C). In a large bowl, mix the first six ingredients together with a fork; drizzle honey on top. Add the stock or bouillon, and mix thoroughly. Knead about ten times. The dough should be stiff but not too stiff to be rolled out. Add more stock if it is too stiff. Roll the dough out so it's $^1/_4$ inch thick. Cut with cookie cutter or into squares with a knife. Place the biscuits on oiled cookie sheets, and brush with egg-milk mixture. Bake in a preheated oven for 40 minutes. Turn off the oven and leave the oven door closed for 3 or 4 hours before removing the biscuits. This will make them very hard (good for the teeth and gums of your pet). Keep a week's supply in a glass jar, and freeze the rest. *Yield:* 6 dozen biscuits.

3
Cosmetics

All-Over Beauty

Women spend a fortune every year on cosmetics. Creams, astringents, pore openers, pore closers, remedies for dry skin, remedies for oily skin—the list goes on and on, and these products are always in demand. We all want to look our best, and a giant industry has flourished because of it. Cosmetics are one of the biggest consumer rip-offs. Up until very recently the manufacturers could have a field day. They weren't required to list ingredients on their products. And the fact is that many of the most expensive cosmetics are made from inexpensive ingredients wrapped in fancy packaging and given elegant names. The less expensive lines are by no means cheap, but they do contain many of the same things and often are better for your skin because they aren't as perfume-laden, perfume being the most common cosmetic allergen. They also may have fewer ingredients, therefore offering less possibilities for allergy. Homemade cosmetics have fewer ingredients yet!

Now that cosmetics manufacturers are required to list ingredients on packages, people who take the time to read the labels may be surprised to discover that their favorite formula is comprised mostly of things they have at home.

MAKING COSMETICS AT HOME

You can make most of your own cosmetics and beauty aids at home for a small fraction of what they cost in the stores, using a few simple ingredients. You have the bonus of knowing what you're putting on your skin.

Although there is virtually nothing in the world to which someone isn't allergic, the substances in our cosmetics are quite safe. We try to use natural ingredients whenever possible. However, there are some preparations that need some chemicals if they're going to be efficient.

The equipment you need to make your cosmetics and bath preparations is, for the most part, things that can be found around the average home, namely measuring cups, measuring spoons, a strainer, cheesecloth, a double boiler, a wooden spoon, and an assortment of bottles and jars with tightly fitting covers.

Here are a few pointers on making your own cosmetics. Alcohol is a main ingredient in many cosmetic preparations. If the formula is for external use, isopropyl alcohol (which is very inexpensive) will work nicely, but for a mouth wash or anything that may be ingested, either accidently or on purpose, use only ethyl alcohol or vodka. Isopropyl alcohol must *never* be taken internally. You may use ethyl alcohol (if it's available in your area) for any recipe calling for alcohol, but it will cost you a bit more. Purchase the 95% alcohol. It may be diluted with water if a lesser strength is desired.

When you blend cosmetics, do it thoroughly. Salts and powder can be stubborn and don't always dissolve readily. Take the time to stir them well until you're sure that they're mixed in. Alcohol breaks down oil, making it easier to mix with other ingredients. In a recipe calling for both oil and alcohol, blend the two of them before adding other ingredients.

R.H.

Be cautious when· you're heating paraffin and other flammable products. We always use a double boiler with hot water in the bottom, because it cuts down the risk of overheating.

You can measure paraffin and other solid masses by displacement. Put some water (say ¼ cup) in the measuring cup, and add the solid. The level of the water in the cup minus the ¼ cup is the measure of the solid. Of course, the water must cover the solid or the measure won't be accurate.

SKIN—THE KEY TO BEAUTY

The most important thing you can do for your skin is to keep it clean and well oiled without making it oily. It's not as easy as it sounds. Many soaps are drying and shouldn't be used on the delicate skin of the face. If you use a beauty bar, be sure you select one with a good pH balance, that is, one that is slightly acid (your skin is slightly acid, too). Rinsing thoroughly is also vitally important. The soap you leave on your skin after careless rinsing clogs pores, enlarging them and often causing flaking.

Oily skin tends to be healthier than dry skin, since the natural oils help protect the skin and keep away wrinkles. The teenager who suffers from blemishes caused by an excessive amount of oil is apt to have nicer skin at thirty-five than her friend who's dry skin was flawless during her teens. The older we get, the less oil our systems produce.

There has been a lot of hoopla about skin preparations with vitamins, minerals, and protein added. The advertisements for many of these products are misleading, to say the least. Vitamins, minerals, and proteins work mainly from the inside out, not the reverse. The amount of vitamin D you'll absorb from a face cream is miniscule. A well-balanced diet is the key to vitamin health and a boon to skin, whether it's oily, dry, or normal.

The pH of a product, however *is* important. The skin, like all of the body, is slightly more acid than it is alkaline. The pH is the ratio of acid to alkaline in a product. Since your body is more acidic, the products you use on it should also be more acidic to protect the natural balance.

CLEANSERS

There are natural cleansers for skin that give it that healthy, clean look and feeling. Either wheat germ oil or avocado oil, both available in most health food stores, do a great job of removing makeup. We personally prefer wheat germ oil because it's so much less expensive than avocado oil, but the advocates of avocado oil feel that their favorite is far superior and well worth the price.

A small amount of oil on a piece of cotton will suffice. If your face is especially grimy or you wear a great deal of makeup, you'll want to go over it twice, turning the cotton as you wipe. When you get to the area surrounding your eyes, pat and dab but do not rub! This part of the face looses its elasticity sooner than the rest of your skin and requires tender, gentle care. When your face is shiny clean, rinse it well with warm water and pat it dry. If you feel this leaves your face too greasy, wash it with a mild, pH balanced beauty bar. Rinse well with warm, never hot, water.

Vegetables and fruits are also natural cleansers. Rubbing your face with the cut side of a potato is a good way to clean oily skin, while an apple, cut up and rubbed over the face, will clean dry skin. But using this method regularly can be expensive (it adds up to a lot of apples or potatoes in a month) and time consuming (the fruit or vegetable juice should be left on at least a half an hour). So we prefer this method only as an occasional change for the skin, say once a week.

Whisk-Away Cream

Here's a makeup remover that can be prepared for future use. This recipe will provide a two-week to one-month supply, depending on how often you change your makeup.

1 tablespoon paraffin wax
1/4 cup beeswax
1/2 cup U.S.P. Grade mineral oil
1 1/2 teaspoons ground camphor

1 tablespoon glycerin
a few drops oil-based perfume (optional)

In the top of a double boiler, over low heat, melt the paraffin and beeswax. Remove the pan from the heat, cool slightly, and add the mineral oil. Mix the camphor and glycerin, and add them to the wax-oil mixture. Add the perfume. Store in a tightly covered jar. Apply a thin layer to your face to remove makeup.

Oily Skin Tonic No. 1

If you have trouble with makeup getting blotchy dark in some places and wearing off in others after it has been applied for a short time, you probably have oily skin and enlarged pores. This formula should help this condition if you use it regularly.

1 teaspoon boric acid powder
1 cup witch hazel

Thoroughly dissolve the boric acid in the witch hazel. Store in a bottle with a tight stopper, and dab on your face with cotton after cleaning your face and before applying makeup.

Oily Skin Tonic No. 2

Another boost for oily skin is this old recipe:

    1 part alcohol
    1 part tincture of benzoin
    1 part white vinegar

Mix ingredients and store in a tightly capped bottle for 10 days before using. Remove about half an ounce, add an equal amount of water to it, and apply to face with cotton. Avoid using around your eyes.

American Beauty Cold Cream

1 cup U.S.P. Grade mineral oil	1 teaspoon boric acid powder
1/2 cup beeswax	3/4 cup hot water
1 tablespoon paraffin	10 drops oil of rose

In the top of a double boiler, put the mineral oil, beeswax, and paraffin. Heat over simmering water until the waxes are melted. Combine the boric acid and hot water; mix well and add the oil of rose. Now pour the water slowly into the wax, stirring constantly. Remove from heat and cool slightly. Store in tightly covered containers. Use as you would any cold cream.

SKIN MASKS

Face lifts may be "in" these days, but they're not only expensive, they're major operations. If you're not up to that, but want to give your face and your spirits a temporary lift, try one of these facials.

Beat two egg whites until they're frothy but not stiff. Apply to face and neck and let dry for about 15 minutes. Rinse off with warm water. Doesn't that make those muscles feel taut!

Whey, that watery substance left from cheesemaking, will accomplish the same thing. Gently massage whey into your skin and leave it on for 15 minutes. Rinse off with warm water. Adding a little lemon juice to the warm rinse and following with a cold water rinse adds zip to this facial.

One of the things in the cupboard that will help dry skin when applied as a mask is mayonnaise. Homemade is best because you can be sure of the purity of the ingredients, and you can make it without mustard, which isn't good for your skin. Leave the mask on for about 15 minutes, wipe it off, and go over your face with warm water.

Honey is a wonderful skin softener and an ingredient in many cosmetic products. A mixture of honey and yogurt in equal parts, applied to the face and left for 15 minutes or so before rinsing off with warm water, is a popular facial mask. Another favorite is honey and light cream used in equal parts and beaten together slightly before applying to the face for 20 minutes. But the honey recipe that we think is a real "honey" is this sweet-smelling facial mask.

Honey-Rose Facial

2 tablespoons rose water	2 egg yolks, beaten
2 tablespoons honey	6 tablespoons flour (approximately)

Heat the rose water just enough so that the honey will dissolve or soften in it; add honey. Cool slightly and add the egg yolks. Slowly add the flour until you have a thick paste. Apply to your face, avoiding the area around your eyes. Leave it on for 20 minutes, then rinse off with warm water. (This may take several minutes, as the flour is not easy to get off. Be persistent but be gentle.) Follow this mask with a lotion or oil.

ASTRINGENTS

What is the role of an astringent? It causes the pores to shrink. In the case of oily skin, where the pores may be enlarged from excessive secretion, an astringent is a must, especially in warm weather. Alcohol, witch hazel, alum, lemon juice, vinegar, and buttermilk all have astringent properties, and one or more of them is a part of many astringent formulas.

One astringent that is very effective is made with hot water and cider vinegar, in equal parts. Apply to the face for about 10 minutes, then rinse well.

The peels of many vegetables and fruits also have astringent qualities. Cucumbers have been used for generations as an astringent and to cool the faces of tired cooks on hot summer days. Try rubbing the peel on your face the next time you're preparing a salad. It provides a delightful pick-me-up! Here's another:

Cucumber Skin Cooler

$1/2$ cucumber, peeled and cubed
1 teaspoon tincture of benzoin
$1/2$ cup rose water

Blend the cucumber in a blender and strain through cheesecloth; discard the pulp. In a tightly covered glass bottle, mix the cucumber juice with the other ingredients. Shake well. Apply to a clean face with cotton.

Bitter-Orange Astringent

If you like an astringent that's pleasant smelling and fairly strong, here's one for you:

$3/4$ cup ethyl alcohol	1 tablespoon glycerin
1 tablespoon witch hazel	4 drops oil of neroli

Add the oil of neroli to the alcohol; mix well. Add the witch hazel and glycerin and store in a tightly capped bottle.

THE WEATHER AND YOUR SKIN

The end of winter seems to find everyone feeling dragged out and haggard, and skin will show it, too. Rub winter-weary elbows, heels, and knees with the cut side of half a lemon. Follow this by a 10-minute soak in warm oil. Sweet almond oil is lovely for this purpose. It has a pleasant scent and makes you feel luxurious. Olive oil will soften your skin, too. You'll look ten years younger (at least around the elbows and knees!).

Another miracle worker on elbows, knees, feet, and hands that are showing signs of wear is a mixture of:

1 cup U.S.P. Grade mineral oil
1/2 cup sesame seed oil

Mix these two together and rub into hardened areas of skin.

Sunbathing should be approached with the utmost caution. Many a sun-worshiper has turned into a wrinkled old lady long before she should. Although the sun's rays do contain vitamin D, they also destroy B vitamins and dry out the skin's natural oils. So before you try for that nice even tan, ask yourself, "Is it worth it?" If the answer is "Yes!" take some precautions.

Fortify yourself with B complex vitamins and lather up with oils to replenish those that the sun will steal. This is an easy lotion to make for that purpose:

Open-Sesame Lotion

3/4 cup sesame seed oil	1/4 cup wheat germ oil
1/2 cup safflower oil	1 teaspoon oil of almond

Mix ingredients together, apply liberally, and don't stay out too long!

If you overdo the sunbathing and you're left with painful blistering skin, cold tea is a soothing comfort. Soak clean cloths or towels in the tea and apply them to the burned area. Cold water is helpful here, too, as it is in the case of any burn, if it's applied soon enough.

The substance found in aloe leaves is a wonderful sunburn remedy. If you live in the south where aloe plants grow, you can collect the leaves yourself. Break the leaf open and rub the milk right onto the sunburned area. Cosmetics manufacturers have become aware of this old-fashioned remedy, and now many of the commercial sunburn lotions contain aloe. A gel made from the milk of the leaves can also be purchased in health food stores.

Skin can become chapped either by windy winters or by summer sun. Whichever is the culprit, the result is uncomfortable. Here are some remedies:

Lip Balm

1/4 cup beeswax
2 tablespoons sesame seed oil
1/4 cup cocoa butter

Heat all ingredients together in the top of a double boiler over simmering water until melted. Stir to blend well, and cool the mixture slightly before storing in a tightly covered jar. Apply generously to chapped or cracked lips.

Thirsty Skin Soother

2 parts glycerin
1 part water

Mix well and apply liberally to chapped hands and face.

A WORD ABOUT FRECKLES

Doris Day has made a fortune with them! But, Doris notwithstanding, most women who have freckles want to get rid of them. And cosmetics companies have tried to oblige them by making creams and lotions purported to make freckles vanish. These preparations are largely unsuccessful in anything but making money for the industry. Freckles are the result of the buildup of melanin (a skin pigment) in one place. Chances are that nothing you do is going to make your freckles go away, but if you're determined, there are a few things that may make them fade slightly.

Winter freckles are more permanent than the ones that appear with the summer sun. One remedy for summer freckles, of course, is to avoid Old Sol. But if you're a sun worshiper, instead of wasting money on freckle creams, try bleaching your spots with buttermilk or lemon juice, both natural bleaches. Don't expect miracles, but constant applications should make them fade a bit. And if they don't, why not agree with most people that freckles can be attractive!

BATHING BEAUTIES

Everyone needs a good all-over, thorough cleaning (in addition to the daily bath or shower) every now and then. Something to get the blood flowing more rapidly and the skin tingling. One way to do this without spending money on abrasive salts is to use plain cornmeal. Wet your facecloth with warm water, wring it out and put about two tablespoons of cornmeal on it. Now give yourself a good rubdown with the facecloth. Makes you feel alive, doesn't it? This is best done just before you take a bath. Add a little baby oil to your bath—it's very soothing after a cornmeal rubdown.

When life has you down, a good relaxing herbal bath can pick you up. A half hour of soaking, and your troubles float right down the drain.

R.H.

Herbal Bath

2 tablespoons dried rosemary
2 tablespoons dried violet leaves
1/2 cup boiling water
1 teaspoon ground camphor
1 cup white vinegar

Steep the rosemary and violet leaves in 1/2 cup boiling water for 5 minutes. Strain and add the liquid to the camphor and vinegar. Pour the liquid in your bath water and relax.

Strawberry Salts

Bath salts, another marvelous bath preparation, are simple and ridiculously inexpensive to make at home. This batch will last you for a long time, and you'll be wondering why you ever spent so much on commercial salts.

1 large (6 or 7 pound) bag of sodium sesquicarbonate
3 teaspoons oil of strawberry
1 1/2 teaspoons oil of sandalwood

Thoroughly mix the oils into the sodium sesquicarbonate. Put the mixture in tightly capped glass jars. Allow it to age a week before using so that scents will mingle with salts. Use about 2 tablespoons of salts in your bath, putting them under the faucet while the water is running.

Oatmeal Bath

This one is recommended for dry or itching skin. Put 1/2 cup raw oatmeal into a blender. Blend on medium-high speed until it reaches the consistency of flour. Sift to remove any unground flakes. To prepare an oatmeal bath, put 2 tablespoons of the oatmeal flour into the tub, and let warm water run full on it. If you wish, a few drops of mineral oil can be added. Soak at least 15 minutes, then rinse.

If you don't have a blender, you can use 1 cup cooked oatmeal tightly tied into a cheesecloth bag. Fix the bag to the faucet so that warm water runs through it as the tub fills.

BATH POWDERS

Bath powder is designed to absorb moisture—the moisture left after your bath and the moisture you're liable to generate before your next bath. Plain cornstarch dusted on the body is adequate for this purpose, but, by itself, it lacks that sweet-perfumed-after-bath feeling. Here's a slight variation on cornstarch that puts it in a class with the most expensive commercial powders.

Sweet-Scented Bath Powder

1 1/2 cups cornstarch
4 drops rose oil
4 drops lavender oil

Mix all ingredients thoroughly and store in a tightly covered container. A cotton pad can be used as a powder puff, or you can splurge and buy a real one at your local five-and-dime store.

Rice Powder

½ cup unscented talcum powder
3 tablespoons boric acid powder
½ cup rice powder

½ teaspoon of your favorite cologne.
(you can make one of the colognes
in the perfume section, see Index).

Mix the first 3 ingredients. Add cologne and mix well. Let the mixture age about a week before using.

Hypo-Allergenic Deodorant

Many people are allergic to the array of antiperspirants offered in the market-places. They can present a real problem. Happily, this may be the solution:

2 cups water
½ cup isopropyl alcohol
1 tablespoon powdered alum

¼ cup lemon juice, freshly squeezed
and strained

Bring water to a boil; remove from heat and add the other ingredients. Bottle in tightly covered jar and apply with a clean cloth to underarms after bathing.

HANDS

Everyone has seen those ads featuring the gals with gorgeous hands that do dishes three times a day. But we don't think you have to use the products they're selling to have young-looking hands. Faithful use of one of the following hand lotions will protect your hands against normal wear and tear.

Orange Lanolin Lotion

2 teaspoons boric acid powder
½ cup petroleum jelly
¼ cup lanolin

¼ teaspoon oil of neroli
3 tablespoons glycerin
⅓ cup water

In the top of a double boiler, heat the boric acid, petroleum jelly, and lanolin until they are well blended. Remove from heat. Mix the glycerin and water together and add it to the first mixture, blending well. Cool slightly, and store in a tightly covered jar.

Violet Hand Lotion

1 tablespoon powdered tragacanth
½ cup water
⅓ cup isopropyl alcohol

1 teaspoon tincture of benzoin
¼ cup glycerin
1 teaspoon extract of orris

Mix the tragacanth in the water. Mix other ingredients together thoroughly and add them to the tragacanth. Store in a tightly covered bottle.

Creme de Almond

This pleasant cream works well on either hands or face.

¼ cup almond oil
½ cup glycerin

1 lump of white beeswax the size of
small lemon
1 cucumber, cubed and peeled

In the top of a double boiler, heat the first three ingredients. Add the cucumber, and simmer for 15 minutes. Strain through a regular strainer. Allow the mixture to cool slightly before bottling in a jar with a tightly fitting lid. Rub into your face and hands before retiring.

No-Nonsense Lotion

If your hands seem really damaged and you want a no-nonsense, get-the-job-done lotion, try this one.

3 tablespoons glycerin	3 tablespoons lanolin
2 tablespoons petroleum jelly	1 tablespoon cocoa butter

In the top of a double boiler, over low heat, melt all ingredients together. Mix well, cool slightly, and store in a tightly covered jar.

THE EYES HAVE IT

Among the first places to show fatigue and age are the eyes and surrounding areas. The natural oils of the skin dissipate more rapidly here than in any other part of the face. A gentle oil treatment of the eyelids and undereyes can be a great boon to preventing tiny lines that soon become crow's feet. Any mild oil will do. Mineral oil, olive oil, and sesame seed oil all work well. No need to purchase expensive eye oils (and they *are* expensive, costing many dollars for a few ounces). Not only are they unnecessary, they can be harmful. Most of them contain perfumes. Since perfumes constitute the largest class of allergens in the cosmetic field and the area usually most susceptible to allergic reaction is the eyes, you can be buying yourself misery. When you're applying oil, cosmetics, or anything else to the eye area, do so with utmost care! Pat, do not rub . . . dab, do not smear. That tissue stretches so easily, and once stretched it doesn't go back.

If you've had a hard day and you're expecting a tired evening because of it, chances are that you can reverse that feeling in half an hour. Tired eyes contribute substantially to an overall tired feeling. So work on your eyes first. We have found that ice cubes wrapped in a face cloth and placed over the eyes for 10 minutes stimulate the circulation and alleviate eyestrain. Lie down while you're waiting for this miracle to occur. (The rest will help, too.) Another thing that makes tired eyes feel better is placing a wet, but not dripping, tea bag on each eye. No need to use a new one for this. The one you used to make your morning tea will do the trick. (Don't use an exotic blend for this, just an ordinary, everyday tea.)

Now you've used 10 minutes of that half hour and you should feel better already. Follow this eye treatment with a relaxing 20-minute bath and you'll be ready for a special evening.

FEET, OR GETTING A KICK OUT OF LIFE

Astrology buffs know that Pisces are ruled by their feet. But you don't have to be a native of that sign to be troubled by your feet. If you do have tired feet, cheer up! There are things you can do to make your feet feel fine again! Walking barefoot, whenever you can, is a wonderful preventive for foot problems, and it certainly makes aching feet feel better to be free. And soaking sore feet can feel close to heavenly!

Tonic for Aching Feet

1 cup epsom salts
1 gallon warm water
a few menthol crystals (optional)

Dissolve the epsom salts in the warm water. Place in a large pan (it must be large enough to accommodate both feet without cramping). If you want a tingly feeling in your feet, add the menthol crystals.

MAKEUP

Most formulas for eye shadow, mascara, and eyeliner are quite complicated, and we don't think they're worth the effort of making. Rouge, face powder, and liquid lipstick are not as difficult. In fact, they're fun to make. The ingredients are mostly things we have in the house for use in other recipes.

Liquid Rouge

1/8 teaspoon cosmetic color of your
   choice
2 tablespoons alcohol

1/4 cup glycerin
1/2 cup rose water

Dissolve the cosmetic color in the alcohol. Add the glycerin, mixing well (this is an important step). Put the rosewater in a bottle that has a tight-fitting lid. Pour in the glycerin mixture, cover, and shake well. Apply sparingly to cheeks with fingers or cotton pad for a radiant glow.

Luscious Lipgloss

5 tablespoons cocoa butter
1 tablespoon beeswax
1/8 tablespoon cosmetic color of your choice

In the top of a double boiler over simmering water, melt the beeswax and cocoa butter, blending well. Remove from heat. Cool slightly, and add cosmetic color. Store in a small, tightly covered jar, and apply with a brush.

Moon-Glow Face Powder

1/2 cup talc
3 tablespoons cornstarch
food coloring, red and yellow (or cosmetic color)

In a medium-sized bowl, mix the talc and cornstarch well with a fork. In a small bowl, put about 1 tablespoon of the mixture. Add a few drops of red color and blend in well with fingers. (This takes a few minutes. Be sure that you have worked the coloring in thoroughly before proceeding with next step.) When powder is an even, bright pink, return it to the rest of the powder and mix it well with a fork. If the powder is too pink or the shade seems a bit off for your complexion, remove another tablespoon of it to small bowl, and blend in a few drops of yellow with your fingers. Return it to the rest of the powder and mix well with a fork. Pack in a shallow jar with a tight-fitting lid.
   Note: Experiment until you get exactly the shade that's right for you.

Here's one for the men:

1 cup water	3 tablespoons glycerin
1/4 teaspoon powdered alum	1/2 cup witch hazel
1/4 cup isopropyl alcohol	1/4 cup rose water or orange water

Heat the water and dissolve the alum in it. Let cool. Add all the other ingredients and mix well. Store in a tightly capped bottle.

Hair Care:
Put the Shine in Your Crowning Glory

Hair is considered part of your skin by the medical profession, which is why you consult a dermatologist if your hair reaches an unhealthy state. Of vital importance to its well-being is the condition of the scalp, where hair follicles (the cells from which hair emerges) determine the rate of growth, abundance, and strength of your tresses.

Nothing you put on your hair can do as much for it as what you put into your stomach. Proper nutrition feeds hair as it does every other part of the body, and adequate circulation in the scalp assures the supply of necessary nutrients to the follicles. Since hair *is* protein, sufficient protein is the number one ingredient in a diet to promote beautiful, thick hair. The B vitamins and trace minerals, especially iodine and zinc, should also be included. One or two tablespoons of salad oil a day (taken in a salad, of course) can help the body fight dry skin, which on the scalp becomes flakes of dandruff. Take care of your general physical health, and you will be taking care of your hair, too.

Nor can mental health be overlooked when it comes to discussing hair condition. The victim of continual stress may find that his or her hair is affected. Lackluster hair, excessive dandruff, and even erratic bald spots can be the result of emotional problems. We have a number of phrases in our language which suggest that the emotions go straight to the scalp, and they are based on truth. "I was so scared my hair stood on end." . . . "That really gets my dander up." . . . and other such idioms describe real effects. One bit of popular hair lore is not true, however. Worry does not cause the hair to turn gray.

Recently, there has been much talk, especially in advertisements, about the pH balance of hair. The pH factor is the scale of acidity/alkalinity. The skin, including the scalp, is protected by an acid mantle that alkaline soaps wash off. After a few hours, the skin restores its acid mantle, but, in the meantime, it lacks some of its natural protection. Special shampoos have been developed which maintain the pH balance of hair. If you use a regular shampoo, however, you can return the acid mantle immediately by using a vinegar or lemon juice rinse after shampooing.

Every chemical process which forces hair to be what nature didn't intend—curly instead of straight, straight instead of curly, blond instead of brunette—destroys some of your hair's natural protection against the elements. It is generally not considered good practice to subject the hair to two chemical processes, such as bleaching and permanenting, at the same time. Like other chemicals, chlorine in swimming pools is bad for hair and should be rinsed out promptly.

Hair is no longer living tissue once it has grown out of the scalp. Therefore, it is easily damaged by rough handling. If rough handling extends to the scalp, the follicles, too, can be damaged, and their ability to replace hair, which is their continual occupation, can be diminished. For example, a tight elastic pulling together a pony tail over a period of months can damage the follicles around the hairline, causing it to recede. Even the tension from snug rollers can damage follicles and cause thinning or small bald spots.

As you can imagine, follicle damage is much worse than chemical damage to the hair strands. As long as the follicles are healthy, just cutting the hair short can remove the evidence of chemical damage. Split ends should be trimmed, anyway, otherwise the split will continue to travel up the hair strand.

What is called "male pattern baldness" occurs at whatever age one's genes decree, and there is as yet no known cure or delay for this natural effect of aging (other than transplants). All that can be done is to keep the hair as healthy as possible to achieve the optimum amount of regrowth that heredity will allow.

All processes applied to the hair should be gently done, from brushing and combing to massage. There is nothing to be gained from one hundred vigorous strokes of the brush every day, other than to prove that your hair can take a lot of abuse. A natural bristle brush is easier on the hair than one with plastic bristles; a wide-tooth comb is preferable to one with closely spaced teeth. Teasing or back-combing causes snarls that break and damage the hair.

Extremes in temperature are rough on hair. Blow-drying daily, for instance, subjects the hair to high temperatures too often, and the result is frequently uncontrollably dry hair. The cosmetic industry has come up with conditioners to improve this situation, but it is far better to blow-dry less often and never to go above the warm setting on the dryer.

With these hair facts in mind, we offer the following recipes which are good for hair, less expensive than their beauty parlor counterparts, and readily available in your own kitchen.

Hot Oil Treatment

This treatment for dry or damaged hair, or for dry scalp, was invented by the ancient Egyptians (who used castor oil). It is still given in beauty parlors today because it effectively restores the shine and glowing good health to hair.

In a small skillet, warm 2 tablespoons of olive oil but don't let it get hot. Test the temperature carefully. *For dry scalp:* With the tips of the fingers, take up as much oil as will adhere to them and rub it gently into the scalp. Repeat this process until the oil is worked into the entire scalp. *For damaged hair:* Concentrate on the hair strands instead of the scalp.

Meanwhile, have a towel soaking in hot water. Wring it out as tightly as possible. Wrap the towel around your head for 20 minutes. Then shampoo as usual, but give the hair extra sudsing to remove the oil.

Hot Honey and Oil Treatment

You may have noticed that there are hair conditioners on the market which use honey, with either milk or wheat germ oil. But honey itself is not a new beauty treatment; it dates back to the Queen of Sheba.

This one is to promote shiny, bouncy hair and to prevent splits and frizzies.

Use 1 tablespoon of honey and 2 teaspoons of olive oil. Proceed as for Hot Oil Treatment.

Egg Shampoo No. 1

For dry, brittle, or chemically damaged hair, use 2 egg yolks, beaten, with 1 tablespoon of your regular shampoo (less if it's a concentrate). Shampoo with *warm not hot water* (you don't want to cook that egg!). Rinse thoroughly.

Egg Shampoo No. 2

For fine, fly-away hair, use 2 egg yolks, but do not add any shampoo. Proceed as for Egg Shampoo No. 1, but massage a little longer than usual. The egg yolk alone will provide the cleansing agent.

Protein Shampoo

This treatment is for lackluster, undernourished hair. In a small saucepan, sprinkle 1 package (1 tablespoon) unflavored gelatin (that's the protein) over 1/2 cup water. Let it set for a few minutes. Then heat and stir until the gelatin dissolves. Mix with 1 cup liquid shampoo, and beat well. Store in a wide-mouthed jar, because the shampoo will thicken.

Dry Shampoo

This is a quick shampoo for campers, cold sufferers, and others for whom a wet shampoo is not convenient. Use about 1/2 cup fine cornmeal. Section off the hair and rub the cornmeal into one section at a time. Brush thoroughly but gently to remove all the cornmeal, which will take with it the dust, dirt, and accumulated oils in your hair.

Grandma's Real Soap Shampoo

To beat the frizzies and pamper dry hair, dilute 1/2 cup White Soft Soap (see page 43) with 1/4 cup hot water. Add 1/2 teaspoon olive oil or coconut oil (coconut oil is lovely but it is harder to find in stores). Use as a shampoo. Follow with a Vinegar Rinse to remove any lingering traces of soap. Grandma used this shampoo with rain water.

Rain Water Shampoo

Because rain water is mineral-free, shampooing in this soft water promotes manageable hair. Anyone who lives in a hard water area might want to try this. Collect rain water in a large enamel basin or pail. Strain it through cheesecloth. Use with a mild shampoo. If you have enough rain water, use it to rinse your hair also.

Vinegar Rinse

This rinse will add highlights to brunette hair, restore the acid mantle, and remove all traces of soap film and hair oil. After shampooing, pour 1/4 cup vinegar into a basin of warm water and rinse your hair in this mixture thoroughly. Notice how soft this makes your hair feel! Rinse again with plain warm water.

Lemon Rinse

To add highlights to blond hair and to do all those other good things that vinegar does for brunette hair, use the juice of 1 lemon strained through cheesecloth. Add this to a basin of warm water and proceed as for Vinegar Rinse.

Sage Rinse

Use this to enhance brunette hair, and just because it smells so nice! Pour 2 cups boiling water over 2 tablespoons dried sage leaves. Allow it to steep and cool. Strain, and use in the final rinse after a shampoo.

Chamomile Rinse

To improve the color of blond hair that is dull and faded, pour 2 cups boiling water over 1/4 cup dried chamomile flowers and leaves. Proceed as for Sage Rinse.

Sage and Black Tea Rinse

For dark hair that is graying, pour 2 cups boiling water over 2 tablespoons dried sage leaves and 2 tablespoons black tea. Proceed as for Sage rinse.

Marigold Rinse

To restore faded blond hair, steep 1/2 cup golden marigold blossoms (loosely packed) in 2 cups boiling water. Allow this to cool and use as a final rinse after shampooing.

Protein Hair Setting Lotion

Towel-dry your hair. Mix 2 tablespoons dry milk with 1/2 cup water, and comb through the hair before setting.

Beer Hair Setting Lotion

Towel-dry your hair. Comb 1/2 cup flat beer through the hair before setting.

Magnesia Hair Setting Lotion

Towel-dry your hair. Mix together 2 tablespoons milk of magnesia, 1 cup water, and a few drops of water-based perfume. Comb through the hair before setting.

Hair Grooming Lotion

This is for anyone who is training short hair to do what it doesn't want to do. In a small saucepan, warm 1/2 cup safflower oil, 1 teaspoon lanolin, and 1 teaspoon castor oil until the lanolin melts. Pour into a bottle, and add 2 tablespoons alcohol. Shake well. Shake *again* every time before using.

Colognes and Other
Sweet-Smelling Things

Since ancient times, men and women have been seeking to seduce each other by appealing to the sense of smell. And we're still at it! Every year finds new scents being added to the already large collection offered. The ads hint that everything from romance to riches will at be the fingertips of the wearer. Who falls for this? . . . We all do! After all, that dab of perfume can add a feeling of luxury to any special evening, and wearing an attractive individual scent can make you feel special any day. Parisians were the first to make perfumery profitable. Their expertise in this field dates back to the 1200s, and, of course, Paris is still the center of the perfume world. Some perfumes seem ridiculously expensive, but often the ingredients number in the hundreds and some of them are so difficult to obtain that the high price is unavoidable.

Making perfume is a complicated art and we'll leave it to the artisans. But making colognes and toilet waters, which we prefer because their odors are lighter, is a great deal easier and vastly cheaper. One of the main differences between perfumes and colognes is the ratio of scented oils to alcohol. A cologne or toilet water contains about 1% to 3% scented oils (the expensive ingredients in perfumery) and the other main ingredient is alcohol. The alcohol used in colognes and toilet waters may be as weak as a 50% solution. The weaker the alcohol percentage, the less expensive the alcohol. You should use Denatured Alcohol, Type 40 or ethyl alcohol for making cologne. Many people use vodka.

Perfume, on the other hand, contains a minimum of 5% scented oils (in the cheaper perfumes) to 20% or 25% scented oils (in the more expensive fragrances). The alcohol is the costlier 95% volume.

COLOGNES

Blending your own scent is like writing a symphony: there should be no discordant notes if it's to be successful. Though the main scent should dominate, it seldom stands alone. A blender, or often many blenders, are added to complement, boost, or subtly change the main scent. Rose, jasmine, orange blossom, and violet are good main scents. They're easy to work with, thus making them excellent choices for the novice cologne maker. You must be careful that the blender you use goes with the main scent, neither conflicting with it nor overpowering it.

Body chemistry must be considered when you select a scent. The perfume that smells divine on one person may not be so pleasing when worn by someone else. Some women like to wear one scent always, like a kind of trademark. If that trademark is a commercial one, however, they are sharing it with thousands of other women. If you want a truly individual aroma for your trade mark, you'll have to concoct it yourself. The more familiar you become with the nuances of scented oils, the more apt you'll be to mix that one scent that you feel is just perfect for you.

When applying perfume, toilet water, or cologne, remember the pressure points you learned about in First Aid. Any place where there is a pressure point is perfect for the application of perfume. The pulse radiates scent rather than keeping it in one spot.

Age all the colognes you make for at least a month before wearing them. This gives the odors a chance to mingle and absorb each other. This aging process should take place in a dark room. The bottles in which the colognes are stored should have extremely tight stoppers to prevent evaporation. If the formula separates after aging, filter it through cheesecloth or a filter paper before using it.

The perfume oils used in our recipes may be found at most health food stores, almost all shops that specialize in herbs, and a few of the real old-fashioned pharmacies. Or, if you'd really like to experiment, try making your own perfume oil. Rose oil is a good one with which to start.

Oil of Rose

1 quart or more of pure safflower oil
rose petals

Put the safflower oil in a shallow pan. Cover the top of the oil with a layer of petals, slightly overlapping each other. Let the petals soak for two days before scooping them off with a slotted spoon. Be careful to scoop off only the petals and not the oil. Repeat this process about 12 times. Each time soak fresh rose petals in the same oil. The scent will become stronger with each application of petals. After the oil is strongly scented, put the oil in a bottle with a tight stopper or cap and store for use in making cologne.

Patchouly Cologne

1¹/₂ teaspoons oil of patchouly
4 drops oil of rose
1¹/₂ cups alcohol

2 tablespoons sandalwood extract
2 tablespoons verbena extract

Dissolve the oils in the alcohol. Add the extracts and bottle the cologne in a container with a tight stopper before aging it.

Spice Island Cologne

10 drops oil of verbena
10 drops oil of neroli
5 drops oil of clove

2 drops oil of cinnamon
5 drops oil of rose
1 cup alcohol

Dissolve the oils in the alcohol. Bottle in a container with tight-fitting cap and store to age.

Florida Water

Variations of this old favorite have been around for a long time.

1 teaspoon oil of lavender
¹/₂ teaspoon oil of lemon
3 drops oil of neroli
¹/₂ teaspoon oil of clove

¹/₈ teaspoon oil of cinnamon
2 cups alcohol
1 cup rose water

Dissolve the oils in the alcohol. Add the rose water, mix well, and store in a tightly stoppered bottle.

Violet Water

¹/₂ teaspoon rose oil
1 cup alcohol
¹/₄ cup violet extract

1 teaspoon cassie extract
2 tablespoons orris extract
2 cups water

Dissolve the rose oil in the alcohol. Add the extracts and mix well. Add water, mix, and store in a tightly stoppered bottle.

If you're ready to go out and find that your supply of cologne has been depleted, or if you just want an everyday scent, look in your kitchen cabinet. Do you have vanilla extract? Try using it as a cologne. You'll be pleasantly surprised. Vanilla extract is an ingredient of many commercial colognes. You might also try some of the other extracts you have for cooking. Almond, orange, and mint are all pleasant smelling. Almond doesn't seem to have the staying power of the others, so even though it smells strong when you first apply it, be generous.

SACHETS

We think it's regrettable that sachets don't enjoy the popularity that they used to. We love to use them. They're ideal to tuck in dresser drawers, hang in closets, and store with linens. Some people even place a small sachet bag in each shoe they keep in their closets.

You can make sachets in any type of aroma you prefer. A sweet scent may seem appropriate for storing with lingerie. You may want to hang a spicy scent with shirts and trousers, and lemon freshness with linens. Whatever you choose, sachets will make your things smell wonderful!

R.H.

All of the ingredients you use in a sachet must be well-dried. Any moisture at all is apt to cause mold and mildew, ruining your sachet and possibly even damaging the items it's intended to scent. Crumble dried flower petals or leaves so that all the scent will be released. Seeds and roots may be worked into a fine powder with a mortar and pestle.

Before you put sachet in bags, let the whole batch age for at least two weeks. This allows the scents to ripen and mingle. Store the batch in a tightly covered container in a dark place and stir it at least once a day.

You need a tightly woven material for making sachet bags. A loose fabric allows the powder in the sachet to leak out. Silk is ideal, and most of the old-time sachet bags were made of it. If you have a fabric that's loosely woven but attractive and you want to use it for sachets, make inner sachet bags from any inexpensive, tightly woven material and cover them with the prettier material you want to show off.

Sachets can be made in all sizes. The perfect size depends on the use. Two-inch square bags are a popular size for use in drawers. But if you're planning to hang your sachet in a closet, perhaps you'll want to make it larger, maybe four to eight inches. The best hanging sachets are made with a double bag. A tightly woven inner bag is covered with an outer bag that's closed with a drawstring, which is used to hang the bag.

Floral Bouquet Sachet

2 cups dried lavender flowers
2 cups dried rose petals
1 cup dried mint leaves

1/2 cup orrisroot powder
5 drops oil of lavender
5 drops oil of rose

Mix all the dried flowers, petals, and leaves. Add the orrisroot and blend well; mix in the oils. Store in a tightly covered container until aged sufficiently to make into sachets.

Spice Rose Sachet

2 cups dried rose petals
1 cup dried patchouly leaves
1 cup ground sandalwood

1/4 teaspoon ground cloves
2 teaspoons oil of rose

Crumble the rose petals and patchouly leaves; mix with the sandalwood and cloves. Add the oil and store in a tightly capped container for two weeks.

Sachet for Linens

This is a modern adaptation of a formula that dates back to the 1700s.

2 tablespoons orrisroot powder
2 tablespoons powdered calamus
2 tablespoons dried lemon peel
2 tablespoons dried orange peel
2 tablespoons dried, crumbled rose petals
1 teaspoon powdered nutmeg
1 teaspoon powdered clove

2 tablespoons dried, crumbled lavender flowers
2 tablespoons dried, crumbled orange leaves
2 tablespoons dried, crumbled walnut leaves
10 drops musk oil

Combine all of the ingredients except the musk oil and mix well. Blend in the musk oil. Put in a tightly covered container to age.

Lovely Lemon Sachet

1 cup dried lemon peel
1/2 cup orrisroot powder

1 teaspoon oil of lemon
1/2 teaspoon oil of bergamot

Mix the dried lemon peel with the orrisroot powder. Stir in the oils thoroughly. Store in a tightly covered jar to age.

This is another way to make things smell nice.

1 orange, lemon, or lime	1 teaspoon ground nutmeg
50 whole cloves (approximately)	1 teaspoon ground allspice
1 tablespoon orrisroot powder	1 teaspoon ground cloves
1 teaspoon ground cinnamon	

Stick the whole cloves into the fruit so that the clove heads are touching. No rind should show, or the fruit will decay. Store in a cool, dry place for four weeks. Roll the fruit in a mixture of all of the powders. Wrap in tissue paper, and put it in closed metal container and store for another week. Remove the pomander ball from the container, unwrap it, and shake off the excess powders. Wrap a ribbon or string around the ball, with a loop at the top so you can hang the fruit in the closet.

Tooth Care:
Smile, Smile, Smile!

The manufacturers of tooth care products have turned them into a billion dollar industry. And, according to the advertisements, there's more to dental hygiene than keeping your teeth functioning. As the various preparations vie for top spot on the hit parade of sales, the promises and subtle half-promises grow . . . better checkups, whiter teeth, sweeter smelling breath, popularity, more dates, and even a better sex life may be yours if you use these products regularly. So convincing are the arguments, that in 1972, the American people succumbed to the sweeter breath promise and spent $240 million on mouthwash alone.

We have found that many dental products can be made right at home. Or you can use things you already have in the cupboard to keep your teeth shiny and your breath sweet. Of course, we are not advocating that anyone forego their semi-annual dental checkup and cleaning—that's a must!

Before you embark on your home program of dental care, you need a proper toothbrush for proper results. Unless you have a problem with your gums, a medium bristle toothbrush is your best bet. If you do have soft or bleeding gums, see your dentist. He may suggest a synthetic bristled brush that's soft and has rounded polished bristles.

Most fruit is great for teeth. An apple a day keeps the dentist as well as the doctor away (or at least it helps to). In fact, an apple is known as "nature's toothbrush" to many dental experts, because biting into one helps get at food that may be lodged between teeth. Strawberries, cherries, and peaches all contain acids that help dissolve the tartar which forms on teeth. If you have a problem with tartar, include these fruits in your diet, and chew them slowly.

Some of us need a good abrasive cleaning between visits to the dentist. An occasional thorough scrubbing with baking soda or salt will remove that dull, dingy look from teeth. But only do this infrequently—about once a month maximum. It can cause damage to tooth enamel.

Tooth Scrubber

This recipe is another good abrasive cleaner for occasional use:

1/2 teaspoon powdered charcoal
1/2 teaspoon precipitated chalk

Mix ingredients and brush teeth, rinsing well after use.

Nicotine Vanisher

If your teeth are stained with nicotine, you might try brushing the stains with pumice powder, or use this recipe:

1/2 teaspoon salt
1/2 teaspoon baking powder
1/2 teaspoon freshly squeezed lemon juice

Mix ingredients well and apply to stained areas of teeth with a toothbrush. Rinse well after brushing. It's important that these substances don't remain on your teeth.

Tropical Toothpaste

1/2 cup precipitated chalk	1/4 cup honey
3 tablespoons orrisroot powder	1/4 teaspoon oil of lemon
1 teaspoon ground cinnamon	1/2 teaspoon ethyl alcohol (50% vol-
1 teaspoon ground cloves	ume)

Mix the chalk, orrisroot powder, cinnamon, and cloves together thoroughly. Add the honey and blend well. Dissolve the oil of lemon in the alcohol and mix into the paste. Store in a tightly covered container.

Wintergreen Toothpaste

1/2 cup precipitated chalk	1/4 teaspoon oil of wintergreen
2 tablespoons orrisroot powder	1/4 teaspoon ethyl alcohol (50% volume)
1/4 cup honey	

Mix the chalk and orrisroot powder; add honey and blend well. Dissolve the oil of wintergreen in the alcohol and mix into the paste. Store in a tightly covered container.

Tough Toothpaste

This one is a bit harsher than the previous two.

3/4 cup powdered pumice	1/3 cup glycerin
1/4 cup orrisroot powder	1/4 teaspoon oil of cinnamon

Combine the pumice and orrisroot powder; mix with the glycerin to form a paste. Add the cinnamon. Store in a tightly covered container.

If you're a toothpowder fancier, there should be one here that you'll like.

Orange Toothpowder

1 cup precipitated chalk	1/2 teaspoon ground cloves
1/4 cup orrisroot powder	1/4 teaspoon oil of orange
1 tablespoon cornstarch	1/4 teaspoon oil of cinnamon

Mix together all the dry ingredients. Work the oils into the powder with the back of a spoon. This step sometimes takes a few minutes and a bit of patience. Store in a tightly covered container in dry place.

Peppermint Toothpowder

This is quite abrasive

1 cup precipitated chalk	2 tablespoons baking powder
1 teaspoon salt	1½ teaspoons oil of peppermint

Mix the dry ingredients well. Work in the peppermint flavoring with the back of a spoon and store in a tightly covered container in a dry place.

Old-Fashioned Toothpowder

1 cup powdered arrowroot	10 drops oil of lemon
3 tablespoons orrisroot powder	5 drops oil of clove

Mix the dry ingredients together. Work in the oils with the back of a spoon.

Denture Cleaner

1 cup warm water
1½ tablespoons sodium perborate

Put the sodium perborate in a cup or glass and add warm water. Put teeth into the mixture immediately, before it's stopped fizzing. Leave the teeth for 5 minutes, then remove them from the mixture and rinse them thoroughly under warm running water.

To keep breath "kissing sweet," chew on a couple of whole cloves or a cardamom seed. Licorice root is another chewy substance that will sweeten your breath, and its advocates recommend swallowing the juice to aid digestion. Other people swear that chewing grains of coffee, sprigs of fresh parsley, or star anise (the Chinese have used it as a breath freshener for centuries) will eliminate breath problems. A breath problem that's related to digestion may be solved by drinking a warm brew of chamomile tea.

Some herbal teas are used cold as mouthwashes. Mint tea is the most popular one. If you want to mix mouthwash that's comparable to the store-bought kind (only cheaper) try one of these:

Citrus Mouthwash

¼ teaspoon oil of lemon	½ cup ethyl alcohol (50% volume)
¼ teaspoon oil of lime	1½ cups water
⅛ teaspoon oil of orange	

Dissolve the oils in the alcohol; add water. Store in a bottle with a tight stopper and shake before using.

Peppermint Mouth Refresher

1/4 teaspoon borax
2 cups water
1/8 teaspoon menthol

1/8 teaspoon oil of peppermint
1/2 teaspoon ethyl alcohol (50% volume)

Mix the borax in water and add the menthol. Dissolve the oil of peppermint in the alcohol and add to the other mixture. Store in a bottle with a tight stopper and shake before using.

Perhaps the best mouthwash of all is plain water. Rinse with it after every meal, especially if you can't brush your teeth. In many areas of our country, water contains fluoride, the substance that's supposed to be the guardian of sound teeth.

4
Home
Remedies

First Aid:
"A Stitch in Time"

We aren't doctors, nor do we pretend any particular expertise in the field of medicine. We do, however, have a few simple, basic measures we use when an ailment or injury is slight, does not require the attention of a physician, or when something has occurred which must be dealt with swiftly and medical aid isn't at hand. Often these measures are preferable to expensive, over-the-counter remedies. In any illness of a serious nature, we recommend treatment by a physician.

Bee and Wasp Stings

Many people are highly allergic to bee stings. If there is a numbness or if the person who has been stung feels dizzy or light headed, or develops hives, medical help is needed at once.

When someone is stung, remove the stinger as soon as possible, and apply a mixture made of ethyl alcohol and ammonia in equal parts. Next, apply ice to the affected area. If pain persists or swelling doesn't abate, get a doctor. If the sting itches, apply plain white vinegar or rub the area with the milk from an aloe leaf.

Black Eyes

If you walk into a door and end up with a shiner, apply cold compresses to the eye as constantly as possible for the first 10 or 12 hours. After this time, switch to warm compresses four or five times daily.

Bleeding

Ice will generally stop minor bleeding. If ice doesn't work, try applying pressure directly to the wound. If bleeding is severe, apply pressure to the pressure point nearest the wound and toward the heart. Only if these methods have failed and bleeding is profuse should a tourniquet be applied. Use a soft material, such as a towel, handkerchief, or necktie, and tighten it between the wound and the heart. Get the patient to a hospital immediately. Don't use a tourniquet for more than 3 minutes at a time without releasing pressure and permitting blood to flow.

It's more important to stop bleeding than it is to cleanse a wound. The fact that it's still bleeding means it's cleansing itself. When you have bleeding under control, or if bleeding is minor, lift out any foreign particles, such as pebbles, with sterilized tweezers. Clean the inside of the wound with a mild soap and water. Rinse with clear water, use alcohol or hydrogen peroxide around, but not in, the wound, and bandage lightly.

Because of their antiseptic properties, onions made into a poultice are a valuable aid for avoiding infection of flesh wounds.

Bleeding Gums

Some people have gums that bleed a bit every time they brush their teeth. To treat this condition, rub the gums with tea bags which have been soaked in cold water. Tea bags will sometimes help stem the bleeding caused when a tooth is pulled, too. Use them like cold compresses. Here's another tried and true help for sore or bleeding gums:

$1/4$ cup water
$1/4$ cup hydrogen peroxide

Rinse the mouth well with this mixture then follow with a rinse of:

$1/8$ teaspoon salt
1 glass of very warm water

Do this several times a day until the condition clears up. If you're still troubled after a week of doing this faithfully, see your dentist.

Blistered Nails

Have you ever hit one of your fingernails with a hammer and had a painful blood blister develop under the nail? Next time this happens, make a small hole in your nail over the blister with a sterile needle or other sharp instrument. This will release the blood and relieve the pressure.

Boils

If a boil doesn't respond well to home treatment, see your doctor. But this remedy works well in many cases:

1 tablespoon boric acid
1 pint hot water

Mix together, and soak clean cloths or gauze pads in the solution. Use as compresses on the boil. Repeat this as often as possible. When the boil comes to a head, it may be opened with a sterile needle. *Don't squeeze it.* Squeezing will spread infection.

Bruises

A vitamin deficiency is often the cause of frequent bruising. If you keep getting bruises that you can't explain, try increasing your daily intake of vitamin C. To treat the bruises you already have, try massaging the area with oil of eucalyptus. When a bruise has just occurred, apply cold compresses to prevent swelling.

Burns

Burn remedies have changed a great deal over the last few years. The medical profession seems to concur now that ice, ice, and more ice is the best emergency measure for any burn, be it first, second, or third degree. If a burn is severe, use the ice treatment only for 10 minutes, then get the patient to a hospital immediately. A patient who is conscious and has just suffered third degree burns should be encouraged to drink water or broth to replace the body fluids that have been lost. A teaspoon of salt added to a quart of water is better than plain water.

Minor burns often hurt more than major ones. The reason for this is that in serious burn cases the nerve endings have been destroyed, lessening the feeling.

But in a burn of a lesser degree, all those nerves are in full play. For a minor burn, it's sometimes advisable to pack it in ice until all pain has subsided. If ice cannot be tolerated, use ice-cold water. This will often prevent any blistering.

A burn of the eye, which has been caused by acid or alkali, should be treated at once by irrigating the eye with plain cool water. After this is done, a physician should be consulted.

Cankers

The same hydrogen peroxide rinse used for bleeding gums (see above) is also good for cankers. Applying alum directly to the affected area usually works wonders, too.

Chill

This remedy works for all parts of the body, including cold feet. It's a great drink when you come in out of a blizzard or when you're chilled through from watching the last football game of the season. If you believe in preventive medicine, try it before you go out on a blustery cold day.

1 cup milk
2 teaspoons honey
$^1/_2$ teaspoon curry powder

Heat the milk almost to boiling. Add other ingredients and stir well.

Colds and Hay Fever

Vitamin C is a well-known natural preventive and remedy for colds and hay fever. 250 milligrams of this vitamin taken four or five times daily should shorten the life of your cold, and if you take vitamin C regularly, all year round, chances are you won't have a cold to cure.

An old-fashioned remedy for hay fever that might relieve you of the pesky problem is 1 tablespoon of honey, gathered from bees in the same area from which come the pollens that are affecting you. This should be taken four times daily.

If a cold seems to have really settled in, this favorite will make the nights more bearable:

1 ounce whiskey
juice of 1 freshly squeezed lemon

$^1/_4$ teaspoon cinnamon (or a cinnamon stick)
2 tablespoons honey

Heat this mixture until it's piping hot. Then drink it down before toddling off to bed.

Diuretics

Dangerous diuretics are taken by millions of people. Among other side effects, they can elevate blood pressure. Before you succumb to the lure of using them, try this simple, natural diuretic. Eat a fourth of a fresh pineapple once a day. In addition to reducing water retention, it will add lots of vitamins to your diet. Fresh, steamed asparagus also has valuable diuretic properties.

Fever Blisters

These annoying sores can't be cured overnight, but there are a few things you can do to make them feel better as they run their course. Witch hazel, dabbed on with a cotton ball at frequent intervals, will help the blisters feel cooler and make you more comfortable. If you have these blisters often, you may want to prepare a mixture of 1 teaspoon of glycerin and $1/2$ cup of witch hazel to have on hand. Keep it tightly sealed.

Hangover

This is said to work better than "the hair of the dog". Blend a cucumber and 1 teaspoon of salt in a blender container. Strain and drink.

Headache

A universal complaint, headaches come in many varieties and with many causes and cures, aspirin being the most commonly used cure. But constant use of aspirin has been known to cause internal bleeding. So, if your headaches are frequent, these methods might work without having to resort to aspirin.

If the headache seems to be centered in the sinuses use:

1 cup vinegar
1 cup of water

Bring the ingredients to a boil in a saucepan. Remove from heat and inhale the fumes from the mixture. This is said to be effective against many headaches of this type.

Tension headaches may respond to a soothing massage of the back of the neck. Place your fingers at the base of the skull, in the center where there's a natural indentation. Massage firmly outward, using equal pressure on each side.

Sinus headaches often let up if you apply pressure to the sinus areas above and below the eyes, toward the nose, just where the bones end. Use a strong circular motion. This may prove to be a bit painful, but continue for a minute or more—it should bring relief. Heat applied to the sinus area often proves beneficial, too.

Hiccups

For some reason everyone seems to smile over a case of hiccups—everyone but the affected person. The so-called remedies are legion. Here are a few of our favorites:

1. Swallow a teaspoon of dry sugar.
2. Mix the juice of one freshly squeezed lemon with a tablespoon of brown sugar. Let mixture dissolve on your tongue.
3. Suck on a sugar cube.
4. Suck on a lemon.

Hives and Prickly Heat

These two different ailments often respond to similar treatments. Try cutting a potato and rubbing the cut side on the affected area. The potato's starch content will relieve the itching from either problem. If the hives are of the giant variety or if they persist, see a doctor. Hives that occur following an insect bite or taking a drug are a cause for alarm; seek immediate medical attention!

Baking soda made into a paste with water and applied to the skin is also good for relief from the itching of hives and prickly heat. Or, if you prefer, you can dust on baking soda instead of making the paste.

Indigestion

Plop, plop, fizz, fizz . . . what you need for indigestion is often an acid, not an antacid. Antacids bring temporary relief, but they compound the problem if it is caused by a lack of stomach acids. Hydrochloric acid tablets may solve the problem completely. They usually bring instant relief from the discomfort of overeating.

Papaya is also an effective remedy for an upset stomach and is particularly good if you have trouble digesting protein.

If you're determined to go the bicarbonate of soda route in an attempt to solve your digestive difficulties, you'll find it goes down easier if you add a few drops of vanilla extract and a teaspoon of sugar.

Insect Bites

For mosquito or fly bites, first apply very cold water or very hot water. Then if they still bother you, try applications of ammonium chloride.

Insomnia

"I didn't sleep a wink last night" is a commonly heard complaint. It's also generally an inaccurate complaint. You may feel like you didn't sleep a wink, but chances are you slept several winks. Sleep does come harder to some of us than to others. But before you reach for sleeping pills, try drinking a glass of warm milk just before retiring. It's been a recommended remedy for generations. A warm bath will often prove soothing enough to make sleep possible. But never take a hot bath, hoping to seduce the sandman—the heat will stimulate you rather than prove soothing. Some herbal teas are great sleep inducers (see "Plant Medicines and Herbal Teas"). But be selective because others are eye-openers.

Itching

For this irritating malady, try freshly squeezed lemon juice diluted slightly with water and applied to the offending area. You may also curb the urge to scratch by lightly dusting a rash or other itching skin with cornstarch or baking soda. Hot water is another effective remedy for itching.

Nausea

That queasy feeling comes over all of us on occasion, and it can often be lessened or overcome by just eating simple foods. Cottage cheese is soothing and so is yogurt. Dry crackers and carbonated beverages often bring almost instant relief. But if the problem is really acute, try slowly drinking the chilled juice from any canned fruit. Some doctors prescribe this for pregnant patients who are suffering from extreme nausea. It really works!

Nose Bleeds

This is another malady with all sorts of antiquated remedies. If you have a nose bleed, don't lie down—stay in a sitting position. First, try to locate where the blood is coming from. If it appears to be from high up, use a cold compress or ice on the back of the neck. If the blood is coming from the middle of the nasal passage, squeeze the nose together tightly in the middle and hold until the bleeding subsides.

Poisoning

The victim of poisoning needs professional advice fast. Immediately call your local poison control center. Try to find out what the patient has swallowed, because the antidote will depend upon that information (although there are universal antidotes used if no information is available about the chemical nature of the poison involved).

The following antidotes are for use only if you cannot contact a poison control center or a doctor for directions.

If the offending substance is ammonia, hydrochloric acid, lye, nitric acid, or oxalic acid, a cup of olive oil can be swallowed.

Vinegar mixed half and half with water should help against ammonia, potassium hydrate, or sodium hydroxide poisoning.

Raw egg white can be quickly swallowed by anyone who's ingested mercury, formaldehyde, lead, or nitric acid.

If the poison is unknown, try a mixture of:

2 tablespoons activated charcoal
2 tablespoons magnesium oxide

Dissolve in one cup of very warm water and drink.

The tendency to induce vomiting is a dangerous one and should be done only if specifically recommended by a physician. In many instances it worsens the situation. Of course, if someone is unconscious, no antidote should be forced. This can only result in choking.

Poison Ivy

There are many new, fancy products on the market to combat this itchy problem. But most of them are no more effective than calamine lotion, and they're all substantially more expensive. If you're looking for a home remedy for this itch, try buttermilk dabbed on with a cotton ball.

Shock

Shock often occurs when there's been a serious injury, and it is identified by cold, clammy skin, loss of color, chills, nausea, and shallow breathing. The injured person should lie down with feet elevated. The patient should be kept covered and, if conscious, given any non-alcoholic beverage to drink. If the injury is an abdominal one, follow all these steps, omitting the intake of liquids.

Sore Throat

Here's a great gargle for a tickly throat:

1 cup water
1/2 cup carageenan
2 tablespoons honey
1/4 cup freshly squeezed lemon juice

Bring the water and Irish Moss to a boil. Remove from heat and allow to stand overnight. Strain, then reheat. Add the other ingredients and mix well.

Warm saltwater is another good gargling solution, as is vinegar and water. If a sore throat persists, or is accompanied by fever, see a doctor.

Sprains

That wonderful cure-all, ice, should be called into action for the first 12 hours after a sprain has occurred. Pack the sprained area in ice and let it rest. Sprains should not be "worked out" as some people believe. The symptoms of sprains and fractures are similar, so, if there's any doubt or if the sprain fails to respond to ice treatment, an X ray is in order.

Sties

Some people are bothered by frequent sties. These may be caused by a number of things (including vitamin deficiency) and should be treated by a physician. For the person who suffers an occasional sty, there are an array of salves and ointments that can be tried in an effort to relieve the pain. We think it's foolish to put any chemical near your eye without the express direction of a doctor. However, if medical help isn't immediately available, try soaking the sty in warm, not hot, compresses several times a day. This should bring the sty to a head. Don't try squeezing it! The heat of the compresses will cause it to break when it's ripe.

Toothache

When you wake up with a toothache and the dentist says he can't see you for two days, try soaking a sterile piece of absorbent cotton in oil of clove and placing it over the offending tooth. This will deaden the pain. If you don't have oil of clove, another old trusted remedy is ginger root. Cut off a piece and chew on it with the aching tooth.

Plant Medicine and Herbal Teas

Great-grandmother had an herb for whatever ailed you, and what could be more soothing when one is feeling "poorly" than a steaming, fragrant cup of herb tea?

As old as the human race, plant medicine was the first medicine, and skilled herbalists were the first physicians. Many of their discoveries were re-discovered in the laboratories of later generations when plant properties could be analyzed, studied, and tested scientifically. Digitalis, for instance, is a product of the foxglove plant. Cortisone was first found in the wild yam and sarsaparilla. Quinine was obtained from cinchona bark. Choline and inositol to lower cholesterol are found naturally in dandelion greens and spinach leaves. And recently, a test in a London hospital found an old African plant remedy, papaya, to be an effective poultice for infected wounds that resist treatment with conventional drugs.

Medicinal herb teas are called tisanes, and they are prepared by decoction or infusion, meaning they are either boiled or steeped in boiling-hot water to extract their essences. A tisane should always be covered while steeping.

A pleasant and useful herb garden can be grown in a relatively small area (even a sunny window, if no backyard space is available). For the beginner, we

R.H.

suggest buying already-started herb plants sold in flats at larger garden centers. Buy seeds only for herbs that are not available in flats, since they can be difficult to start. Note which of your purchases are annuals (which will last one year only) and which are perennial (which will come up every year). Make a sketch of your herb garden area, and mark where each kind of plant is located so that you will be able to identify them accurately and protect your perennials when they spring up again the following year.

Avoid commercial insecticides, and use natural nontoxic ones instead (see page 52) to keep the pests from chewing up your basil and sage. Companion planting is another device we use to keep our herbs bug-free. An edging of marigolds (very pretty!) discourages many garden pests with the marigold's strong odor. Garlic, shallot, and chive plants strategically located among the other herbs perform the same service.

Two herbs are best isolated: greedy mint, because it takes over the space of other plants, and alluring catnip, because it may attract a neighborhood cat, and you won't want your whole herb supply wrecked by a marauding feline.

Fresh herbs can be dried for winter use. First wash them in salted water, then in fresh water. Shake off the excess moisture. Lay them out on clean window screens so that the air can circulate freely on all sides. Choose a hot sunny day, and put the screens outdoors on a table, but not in the direct sunlight. For a smaller harvest, another method is to tie small bundles (3 sprigs) with the twist ties that come with plastic bags, and string the bundles on a line in a breezy open window. (The scent of drying herbs is delectable!) Never dry them in an oven, since this method wastes much of their aromatic essence.

Herb teas are not meant to replace doctors and prescribed medicine, but they may very well be used in place of many over-the-counter drugs of questionable effectiveness and numerous side effects.

ANISE

First grown in ancient Egypt, anise soon earned a reputation as a sedative, a breath-sweetener, and an herb to prevent indigestion. For this reason, the Romans made anise-flavored cakes to serve after a rich banquet. Anise is also recommended by herbalists to quiet a cough or to allay the pains of rheumatism.

Soothing Anise Tea

1 teaspoon anise seed
1 cup boiling water
1 teaspoon honey

Steep the anise seeds in the water for 10 minutes. Strain and add honey.

BALM

Celebrated for its restorative powers, this old-time tranquilizer is believed to improve digestion, circulation, memory, and awareness. It is particularly to be recommended to those who feel heavy in spirit and need to be brightened up.

Balm Tea for a Brighter Outlook

Pour 1 cup boiling water over 2 tablespoons fresh balm leaves. Steep 10 minutes, strain, and serve with a lemon slice.

Balm Cup for Wounded Spirits

1 cup dry red wine
1 teaspoon honey
pinch of ground cloves

1 lemon slice
2 tablespoons fresh balm leaves

In a small saucepan, simmer the wine with the honey, cloves, lemon, and balm leaves for 5 minutes. Strain. Makes 2 servings.

BASIL

"Eat Basil, and be Merry and Glad" the ancients said, for this delicate herb has the reputation of promoting cheerfulness and a good disposition. Time out for a cup of hot basil tea is sure to cheer up a depressed day.

Hot Basil Tea

Steep 2 tablespoons fresh basil or 1 teaspoon dried basil leaves in 1 cup boiling-hot water. Strain, and serve with a lemon slice.

Basil Iced Tea

Fill a glass with ice. Pour over it freshly made, slightly cooled strong tea. Crush 4 or 5 leaves of basil between the fingers and add to the tea. Stir. Serve with lemon, and a sweetener, if desired.

CHAMOMILE

Chamomile is sometimes called "the plant's physician" because plants growing near it seem to thrive especially well. The herb has a long history in folk medicine as a sedative. It's taken to prevent insomnia and even to avoid nightmares. The apple flavor of chamomile makes it one of the most refreshing of herb teas.

Sweet Dreams Chamomile Tea

Bring 1 cup water to a boil. Drop in 1 tablespoon freshly washed chamomile flowers or 1 teaspoon dried flowers. Cover, and let steep 5 minutes. Strain.

CARAWAY

Early American settlers ate caraway seeds with their bread and butter every day to prevent hysterics. (The times were hectic!)

Calming Caraway Tea

1 cup boiling water
1 teaspoon caraway seeds
1 teaspoon brown sugar

Pour the water over the caraway seeds. Allow this to steep for 10 minutes. Strain, and sweeten with brown sugar, if desired.

COMFREY

Also known as knit-bone and boneset, comfrey is reputed to be an all-purpose healing herb ("good for what ails you"), which may be because it's rich in calcium, potassium, phosphorus, plus vitamins A and C. The American Indians used this herb in many ways. Among the Creeks, a tisane of comfrey was given for bodily pain. The Iroquois favored it for fevers and colds, and the Menominees, too, employed it to soothe a fever. The Alabamas treated stomachache with comfrey. Comfrey is usually harvested for tisanes in August. Drink it to your very good health!

Comfrey Tea

Steep 2 tablespoons fresh comfrey or 1 teaspoon dried comfrey leaves in 1 cup boiling-hot water for 10 minutes. Strain. Sweeten with honey, if desired.

CATNIP

This isn't just for cats! Centuries ago, in Europe, it was taken to foster courage or to awaken appetite. The Mohegan Indians used a tisane of catnip to relieve infant colic and popularized it among the English colonists. Today it is listed in pharmacopoeias as mildly stimulating. Cats, however, find it *very* stimulating!

Catnip Tea for Two

Warm a small teapot with hot water. Drain. Put ¼ cup loosely packed, freshly washed catnip leaves into the pot, and pour over them 2 cups boiling water. Cover tightly, and let steep 5 minutes. Strain, and serve with slices of lemon.

DILL

Herbalists recommend dill as a stimulant. Colonial children used to be encouraged to chew dill seeds during long church services to keep them awake.

Bright Eyes Dill Tea

Pour 1 cup boiling water over 1 teaspoon dill seeds. Allow this to steep for 10 minutes. Strain and serve.

FENNEL

Pliny listed twenty-two disorders that could be cured by the use of fennel. Here are two uses for the plant that have been recommended continually since then.

The dried hair (tops) of fennel has flea-repellant properties, which is why the Romans strewed it freely throughout their bedrooms. Since it is nontoxic to humans or pets, you may want to consider using the Pet Powder made with fennel (see page 55). We've also used dried fennel to brush through our dogs' fur when grooming them. The scent is very pleasant.

Secondly, since the days of ancient Greece, a broth of fennel has been used by dieters to quiet the pangs of hunger. The Greeks called the herb *marathon*, derived from *maraino*, meaning "to grow thin." Raw fennel is delicious, low-calorie, and filling, something like a licorice-flavored celery. Or, you can make the following tisane:

Fennel Tea

1 teaspoon fennel seeds
1 cup boiling water
$1/2$ teaspoon honey

Steep the fennel seeds in the water for 10 minutes. Strain and sweeten with the honey.

GINGER

The Chinese have used ginger to quiet an upset stomach, and it has been used by Western herbalists to relieve menstrual cramps.

Fresh Ginger Root Tea

1 slice fresh ginger root   2 cups boiling water
1 teabag   brown sugar and lemon

Dice the ginger root. Warm a small teapot with hot water and drain it. Put the ginger root in the pot with the teabag. Pour the boiling water into the pot, and allow this to steep for 3 minutes. Strain, and serve. Sweeten with brown sugar, if desired, and serve with lemon slices.

LINDEN BLOSSOMS

The French use linden blossoms to make a digestive tonic, the well-known *Til-leul*, taken just before retiring.

Linden Blossom Tea

Pour 1 cup boiling water over 2 teaspoons dried linden blossoms. Let steep 5 minutes. Strain and serve.

MINT

There are over forty varieties of mint, all enthusiastic and aromatic. Mint is a real breath sweetener, and essences of peppermint and spearmint are found in many breath sprays, toothpastes, and chewing gums. As medicine, the mints are used chiefly for feverish colds and flu, as well as for stomachaches. Peppermint oil is recognized as a medicinal agent to relieve the stomach and intestines of gas, and as a stimulant. Irish doctors recommend mint as a cheering-up herb.

Cooling Mint Tea

Pour 1 cup boiling water over ¼ cup fresh mint leaves or 1 tablespoon dried mint leaves. Allow this to steep for 10 minutes. Strain. Serve with a slice of lemon. A teaspoon of honey may be added.

Peppermint Milk

In a small saucepan, heat but do not boil 1 cup milk with ¼ cup fresh peppermint or 1 tablespoon dried peppermint leaves. Turn off heat; allow this to steep for 5 minutes. Strain, and serve as a stomach soother.

NASTURTIUM

The leaves of this plant taste much like watercress and are a nice addition to salads. The blossoms can be eaten, also. The seeds are pickled to use like capers. Known as an herbal antibiotic in the Germanic countries, much as garlic is known around the Mediterranean, nasturtium is rich in vitamin C.

Nasturtium Tea for Two

Pour 2 cups boiling water over ¼ cup chopped fresh young nasturtium leaves. Let steep for 10 minutes. Strain, sweeten with honey, and serve. For an aesthetic experience, wash 2 nasturtium blossoms in salted water, rinse in fresh water, and float one blossom in each cup.

NUTMEG

Nutmeg is a narcotic in large doses. In small ones, it is used to quiet a nervous stomach or headache and also as an insomnia cure.

Sleepytime Nog

1 cup milk	⅛ teaspoon nutmeg
1 teaspoon honey	brandy or sherry (optional)

Heat but do not boil the milk; stir in the honey. Pour into a cup and sprinkle with the nutmeg. If desired, flavor with brandy or sherry.

ROSE HIPS

The fruit of the beautiful wild briar rose is rich in vitamin C. Controversy rages as to whether this vitamin is indeed useful in treating the elusive "untreatable" common cold. Personally, we find vitamin C more helpful than any so-called "cold remedy" on the market.

Rose Hip Tea

2 small rose hips
1 cup boiling water
1 teaspoon honey

Break open the rose hips and cover them with the water. Allow them to steep 10 minutes. Strain, and sweeten with the honey.

SAGE

Its Latin name *salvia* means "heal," and it is a traditional medicinal plant, as well as the friend of turkey stuffings. It makes a delightful house plant, requiring only rich but well-aerated soil, a little water, and constant pinching back. As a house plant, it can provide the time-honored spring tonic and an after-dinner indigestion cure that is always right at your fingertips.

Sage Tea

Pour 1 cup boiling water over 2 tablespoons fresh sage or 1 teaspoon dried sage leaves (do not substitute ground sage for tea). Cover, and let steep for 5 minutes. Strain. Sweeten with honey, if desired.

THYME

Known as a stimulant, thyme is recommended for everything from general depression to hangover and/or headache. The strong aroma of thyme perks up the spirits in a very special way. Try the following tisane:

Perky Thyme Tea

Warm a small teapot with hot water. Drain. Put 2 tablespoons fresh thyme or 1 teaspoon dried thyme leaves in the pot. Add 1 cup boiling water, and steep 5 minutes. Strain and serve. Sweeten with honey, if desired.

WATERCRESS

Watercress is one herb that likes "wet feet," and you can grow watercress in a few days' time on a wet paper towel in the kitchen window. It is difficult to grow outdoors except in a marshy area. Because of its high iron content (plus vitamins A and C), it is recommended for anemia.

Watercress Sandwich

Chop ½ cup freshly picked watercress leaves, and lay them between 2 slices of buttered bread.

Medicinal Foods

Certain fruits and vegetables are medicinal as well as nourishing, and their reputation as healers enjoys the overwhelming testimony of time—and science, in many cases. While we don't suggest they should replace the expertise of modern medicine, we do not forget that some modern medicines are derived from vegetable sources. Although they were discovered centuries ago in trial and error fashion, these foods, repeatedly associated with prevention and cure, have become permanently established in the folk medicine of many peoples. Some foods, once believed to have magical powers, have even become scientifically respectable in the light of recent evidence.

R.H.

The Mythic Apple

A figure in many legends, from the tempting apple of Eden to the golden apples of Greece, this crisp sweet fruit is rich in pectin, which is officially recognized as a drug and used in pharmaceutical preparations. Raw apple juice is alkaline in reaction, and unsweetened natural cider is reputed to be a kidney stone preventive.

Kaopectate, a well-known commercial medicine for the treatment of diarrhea, contains two therapeutic ingredients, one of which is pectin, and the other kaolin, a protective and soothing white clay. Pectin aids detoxification and, as an absorbent, also helps the coating action of kaolin. Obtained from the inner portion of apple peelings, pectin in old-time remedies for diarrhea was extracted by boiling apple parings in milk.

A study conducted at Michigan State University indicated that students who eat two apples a day have fewer tensions, headaches, and emotional upsets than those who eat none. Coincidentally, apples have been prescribed to lower cholesterol and to prevent myocardial infarcts. (Not one apple a day, but two!) Since apples help the body to absorb iron, this fruit has also been used in the treatment of anemia.

The apple is praised by dentists as a perfect detergent food which both stimulates the gums and cleans out debris between the teeth. For those who can't brush after every meal, eating an apple instead can solve the problem.

Not only that, but they taste good, too! A delicious dish to begin your day with is *meusli*, the Swiss cereal. To make it, soak oats or cracked wheat in cold water overnight (one part cereal to three parts water) and then combine it with coarsely grated apple, honey, ground almonds, a little lemon juice, and a dash of cinnamon.

Ubiquitous Garlic

This fragrant bulb, once worshiped by the ancient Egyptians, has been endorsed by centuries of European peasants as a preventative to infectious diseases. Whether it really does have antibacterial qualities is a matter of some dispute, with the pro-garlic faction using it to ward off colds and flu. In folk medicine, garlic has also been used as an expectorant in a syrup to alleviate bronchial coughs and asthma, and as a preventative and/or treatment for worms, as well as an antibiotic.

In recent medical literature, there have been favorable reports of garlic opening up the blood vessels and thus helping to reduce high blood pressure, as well as reports of its being a quieting agent for nervous stomachs.

If, when the flu season descends upon you, you wish to try the garlic prevention system, you can enjoy a minced clove by sautéing it in olive oil as a dressing for thin spaghetti. Add lots of chopped raw parsley, which is not only rich in vitamins A and C, but also in chlorophyl to sweeten the breath.

The Pungent Onion

In folk medicine, the onion is an all-purpose remedy, being known as an aphrodisiac, a narcotic, a hair growth stimulator, and a tonic for bronchial complaints. An old-time cough remedy consisted of half onion juice and half honey.

Onions are considered a good food for the diabetic and the obese, since they lower the blood sugar level. It is also a diuretic and an anti-cholesterol.

The Lovely Lemon

This tart fruit has two special properties. It's antiseptic, which means it helps kill some of the bacteria that may be present in the seafood it's squeezed on, such as raw shellfish, and it's hypotensive, meaning it works against hypertension (high blood pressure).

Lemon is used topically as a skin bleach to lighten dark areas of the skin, such as freckles or so-called liver spots. Historically, it was used as an anti-scurvy remedy in the days before the necessity for vitamin C in the diet was known. Largely by trial and error, it was found that either a lemon or a lime every day would stave off the effects of this disease, the scourge of sailors.

Being rich in vitamin C, a hot lemonade sweetened with honey is a pleasant drink when you feel a cold coming on. In folk medicine, this drink was considered especially efficacious for that scratchy sore throat which often accompanies the onset of a cold. (In truth, a jigger of rum was often added. If you check the ingredients in a number of nighttime cold remedies on the commercial market, you'll find a substantial amount of alcohol included.)

The Philosophic Fig

Called by Plato "the philosopher's friend" because they "strengthened the intelligence," figs have been used to calm a nervous disposition, in a gargle for sore throats (boiled in milk), and to relieve constipation.

Today, it is known that figs and other dried fruits are an excellent remedy for constipation not caused by any disease but resulting from incorrect diet. Eating laxative foods is a far healthier treatment for irregularity than continually taking commercial laxatives, which may create an unhappy and unnecessary dependence.

Because they supply bulk, whole fruits, dried or fresh, are better than fruit juices in correcting constipation.

Try diced dried figs in hot wheat or bran cereal, in place of any other sweetener (figs are quite sweet). Whole grain foods also provide the high fiber that is known to promote regularity.

Remarkable Rice

Another staple food, especially in the Orient, rice is, of course, most nutritious when unrefined. Brown rice is high in the B vitamins and many essential minerals.

Because it is easily digested, rice is an excellent food in cases of stomach and kidney disorders, such as nephritis. Rice gruel or rice water is an old-time remedy for intestinal irritation. It is prepared by cooking the rice until it is reduced to a soft cereal consistency which, when cooled, forms a jelly. Veterinarians often recommend a diet of rice and boiled hamburg for dogs who suffer from diarrhea.

The rice diet, used by Dr. Walter Kemper of Duke University in the treatment of diseases of the blood vessels (high blood pressure and hardening of the arteries), was successful in reducing blood cholesterol in a study of 1,000 patients. The rice diet was based on the theory that it was desirable for these patients to eat foods low in salt, protein, and fat, so unsalted rice was used to make up the bulk of the diet.

The Zesty Radish

Known as an expectorant, respiratory stimulant, diuretic, and nerve sedative, this hot red root is another natural cold fighter. The juice of radishes has also been used to prevent the formation of gallstones by past generations. A favorite among many peasant peoples, the radish is especially prized in Russia as an appetizer, thinly sliced and mixed with sour cream.

Sweet Strawberries

A high content of salicylic acid makes this delectable fruit beneficial to persons with rheumatism. Strawberries have been prescribed for high blood pressure patients, and, because the berries are rich in iron (with almost as much of the mineral as raisins have), they are an excellent food for those suffering from anemia.

In folk medicine, they have been used for centuries as a treatment for gouty rheumatism and whenever toxins were thought to be present in the blood.

Cooling Raspberries

Raspberries are especially recommended by herbalists—along with other acid fruits—for a feverish patient. To make a decoction, boil equal amounts of ripe raspberries and water until the berries are soft (about 5 minutes). Strain. Sweeten, if desired, and chill the juice to use as a cooling drink.

The Native American Cranberry

This tasty food contains a combination of fruit acids considered to be beneficial for urinary infections.

Mild-Mannered Lettuce

This leafy green queen of salads is known for its natural narcotic and gentle nerve-calming properties. In folk medicine, it has been used in the treatment of insomnia. After a hectic day, finely shredded lettuce cooked in chicken broth can be calming to your nerves.

The Sturdy Cabbage

A staple food of generations of lusty peasants, the cabbage was best known in folk medicine for its beneficial effect upon all bronchial afflictions, for which the juice was prescribed. Eaten raw, it is very rich in vitamin C and compares favorably with citrus fruits in that regard. It was one of the foods used to prevent scurvy among sailors of past generations.

In recent medical history, a study done at Stanford University School of Medicine indicated that cabbage juice concentrate speeded up the healing of peptic ulcers to one-third the usual time required with standard treatment. An anti-ulcer factor present in cabbage—and in other fresh greens and cereal grasses—was thought to be responsible for the improvement in healing.

Cabbage loses some of its potency when cooked, so it is best eaten raw, in cole slaw or other salads. Fresh cabbage juice can be prepared easily in an electric juicer or blender.

The Colorful Carrot

Rich in vitamins A and D, the carrot is another known cold fighter and is thought to be beneficial to the complexion. In folk medicine, the vegetable has been prescribed to improve night vision, as a food remedy for liver complaints, and to build up the blood. Carrot increases the number of red blood corpuscles in the body.

Grated carrot is a pleasant addition to cole slaw. Fresh carrot juice is a healthful drink taken in moderate amounts, but too much can be toxic. One glassful in any one day is plenty!

Celery, Tonic for Jangled Nerves

Famous throughout the ages as a tonic for nervous headache, nervous stomach, and insomnia, the "magic" of celery may be its high proportion of vitamins—it contains much vitamin A, vitamin C, and the B vitamins, as well as many essential minerals, including both iron and potassium. At any rate, there are two time-honored ways of benefiting from celery's curative powers: one is to eat a lot of the stuff raw, and the other is to prepare a tisane (or tea) of the seeds. For insomnia, herbalists combine 1/4 teaspoon celery seeds with 1/2 teaspoon anise seeds steeped in a cup of hot water for 10 minutes.

Milk, Nature's Sleep Potion

A solid food in liquid form (it turns to a solid as soon as it's in your stomach), milk is the real nutrition behind all those instant breakfast drinks. And it's even better at bedtime! Milk is a sleep-inducer with more modern medical approval than any of the over-the-counter sleeping aids on the market.

According to an article in the editorial section of the *Journal of the American Medical Association*, a natural amino acid, tryptophan, promotes sleep with little or no effect on the actual sleep stages, whereas sleep-inducing drugs alter the normal sleep patterns by decreasing the time spent in dreaming. Dreaming has psychological benefits and is necessary if sleep is to be refreshing to the mind as well as to the body. It is thought that milk elevates tryptophan levels in the brain.

A cup of warm milk with a teaspoon of honey dissolved in it is our favorite cure for midnight wakefulness.

Coffee and Tea, Natural Stimulants

Caffeine, contained in coffee and black tea, is a stimulating drug used in a number of over-the-counter medicines for different purposes to counteract the effects of other drugs that cause sleepiness, such as antihistamines; in medicines for the relief of menstrual discomforts; in several "extra strength" pain relievers; and all by itself in a pill designed to keep you awake during a long drive or the night before an exam when you want to study.

Although it's unfashionable to have anything nice to say about caffeine these days, when dozing is dangerous or unwelcome, a cup or two of black coffee is a safe, quick, available, and cheap remedy, much more desirable than the over-the-counter pill on which it is just too easy to overdose.

Tea's tannin content is reported to be helpful in cases of diarrhea, while its liquid replaces fluids lost by the body. Tea and dry toast is an excellent diet when recovering from this affliction.

In folk medicine, black tea is the favored drink for soothing migraine, for stimulating mental alertness, and for combating "the blues." Try it with honey and a slice of lemon on a dreary rainy afternoon when the world looks glum.

Nostalgia question: Does anyone remember "cambric tea"? That was the children's tea our mothers used to make. Its chief ingredient was warm milk, but it was flavored with weak tea and sugar and served in a regular teacup. This, too, was a rainy-day antidote.

Wine Tastes Better Than Geritol

Wine is one of the oldest medicines known to man, and its virtues have been rediscovered in recent times. Red wine is especially rich in iron in the ferrous form, which is most readily absorbed by the body. Both red and white wines contain all thirteen of the essential minerals.

Rich in the B vitamins, wine is a natural sedative. About sixty American hospitals serve wine on a doctor's prescription, and it has proved especially beneficial in geriatrics, reducing tension and complaints in older patients. Wine also aids digestion by increasing salivary secretions and stimulating gastric juices. The enzymes it contains are very similar to those in the digestive juices.

For those on a salt-free diet, wine is much lower in sodium content than many other beverages, especially milk. And, according to some diet researchers, moderate amounts of white wine served with a diet regimen help to promote weight loss.

When traveling in foreign countries whose sanitation methods are suspect, it is safer to drink wine than to drink water. Or, as it says in the Bible, "Use a little wine for thy stomach's sake. . . ." (I Timothy 5:23).

Three communities in the world can boast of having the longest living peoples, folks who not only often reach the ripe old age of one hundred years, but also remain hale and hearty, able to work and play with vigor. Their incidence of heart disease and all manner of intestinal diseases is much lower than ours. The three communities are widely separated—the Vilcabambans in the Ecuadorian Andes, the Pakistani Hunzas, and the Soviet Georgians—but they do have several things in common. All are isolated communities, located at high altitudes. All are hard-working peoples. All are proud of their old folks, treating them as a valued and important part of the community. And they have in common, too, the same kind of diet, now being studied by scientists from all over the world.

Homegrown vegetables and fruits (among the Hunzas, apricots are in special abundance as a staple), whole grain cereals, nuts, and dairy products (particularly yogurt, buttermilk, and low-fat cheeses) provide the bulk of their diet. Only a small amount of meat is eaten, and the total daily intake of calories averages between 1,200 and 1,900 calories (as opposed to our average, around 3,000 calories).

Better than any tonic for "tired blood" or the entire dazzling array of drugstore remedies to keep the over-forty crowd regular and peppy, healthy longevity can be promoted by emphasizing these natural-fiber, low-cholesterol foods and adopting the moderation with which they are enjoyed.

Assembling Medical Supplies— Without Going Broke

Most medicine cabinets are already full, but few contain the necessities for competent first aid. The clutter in the medicine cabinet usually consists of old prescriptions, over-the-counter remedies to relieve everything from headache to foot itch, and cosmetic preparations such as mouthwashes and deodorants. It's all too easy to lose sight of the essentials amid the confusion of nose sprays, tiny time pills, and corn plasters.

The number one essential may be to make room for necesssities. If so, you can begin by throwing away all old prescriptions, as medical authorities agree you should. When a serious ailment occurs, you should get a new prescription, if necessary, and not play doctor and dose yourself from the assortment of old prescriptions on hand. Some lose strength from storage; some gain it through evaporation. If it's an antibiotic, there will not be enough left to see you through the course of a sore throat or other illness properly. Nor are they handy to prescribe to sick friends, unless, of course, you happen to be an M.D. Throwing away old prescriptions does not mean dumping them in the wastebasket, by the way. The proper way to dispose of them is either to pour them down the sink, if a liquid, or flush them down the toilet, if tablets. That way you have the security of knowing that no child or pet is going to sample them experimentally.

Another way to make room is to separate the medical supplies from the cosmetic. It could be that the best place to keep medicines is not the bathroom at all but a special cabinet elsewhere in the house. Wherever you keep them, it is just confusing the matter to have to sort through hair sprays and astringents to find a bandage, which you may have to do one-handed if the other hand happens to be bleeding at the time.

Having made room, you are ready to check your stock of necessities in an orderly fashion.

Pain Relievers

Your medicine cabinet should include a pain reliever. Among those available without a prescription, there is none stronger than plain aspirin. If aspirin is what you plan to use, there's no advantage to buying a brand name when you can buy a house brand (both chain drugstores and supermarkets have them) for less money. A regular aspirin tablet by any name will contain 5 grains of the drug.

Although excellent for relieving pain, aspirin does cause irritation to the stomach, which some people can tolerate and some can't. Whether aspirin tablets seem to bother you or not, it's wise to take them with milk rather than water, because milk is a natural buffer.

If you can't take aspirin even with milk, you can try what is called a buffered aspirin, which costs a bit more. It contains aluminum magnesium to offset the irritation caused by plain aspirin.

For a certain number of people, no aspirin, buffered or not, can be tolerated by their systems. (People who have ulcers or asthma should not use aspirin anyway.) These sensitive folk can take three other pain relievers, known as aspirin substitutes: acetaminophen, salicylamide, or phenacetin.

Acetaminophen is available in house brands, too, labeled "non-aspirin pain reliever" or "pain-relief without aspirin." This is the cheapest way to buy it, and it's the same acetaminophen which is also available in more expensive brand names such as Tylenol. Both kinds of tablets contain 325 mg (5 gr) of the drug. Acetaminophen will do everything that aspirin does except relieve inflammation.

Phenacetin will also reduce pain and fever but will not relieve inflammation. It has the possible side effect of kidney damage if taken in excessive dosages. What is excessive differs with different people. Phenacetin is found in combination pills.

Salicylamide will do everything that aspirin does *including* relieve inflammation. It, too, is found in combination pills.

We like to keep both aspirin and an aspirin substitute in the medicine cabinet. When headache or other pain is accompanied by an upset stomach, we can take the substitute so as not to make that stomach feel any worse. When inflammation is part of the problem, as with a strained muscle, we have aspirin to offer relief from both the pain and the inflammation.

Aspirin works faster if it is crushed before taking, although it takes a stoic to abide the taste. If you want to try this, put the crushed aspirin in a teaspoon of honey for easier swallowing.

When you hurt, the phrase "extra-strength pain reliever" sounds very tempting. Many times, this phrase is used in advertisements for a combination pill containing aspirin and one or more of the other pain relievers mentioned above. The combination pill may also contain caffeine. But there is no mysterious extra ingredient; just read the labels. Take, for example, Excedrin. It contains aspirin, acetaminophen, salicylamide, and caffeine. Much like chopping up a few pills and adding a cup of coffee. There is no good reason to waste your money on a combination pill.

The reason that caffeine is frequently added to headache remedies is that it

[155]
Assembling
Medical
Supplies—
Without Going
Broke

stimulates the muscles and the higher nervous system. One cup of ordinary coffee also contains 1½ to 2 grains caffeine.

Time-released aspirin is different from regular aspirin only in that it contains 10 grains per tablet and is supposed to give relief that lasts eight hours instead of four. There is no way to guarantee that your individual body won't absorb the drug faster or slower than intended by the manufacturer, however. It's probably better to take regular aspirin as needed every four hours. If you're asleep and don't wake up to take those extra two aspirin, you didn't need them anyway.

Topical Pain Relievers

When you play too many sets of tennis one weekend, weed the entire garden, or otherwise engage in activities that come as a surprise to your muscles, you may want more than a pain-relieving pill; you may want topical relief, too.

Since inflammation may be involved, aspirin is the ideal internal medicine. Externally, you can apply a heating pad or you can buy a muscle rub. Such liniments work by irritating the skin and bringing the blood to the surface where its warmth acts to relieve the muscle ache. Some liniments also contain an analgesic which is absorbed through the skin. A muscle rub usually provides more relief than a heating pad. If exercising excesses are a frequent occurrence at your house, you may want to have such a muscle rub on hand. Always be careful to keep it out of the eyes and other sensitive areas, because it is an irritant. Wash your hands well in hot water after applying.

A muscle liniment containing oil of wintergreen will give both heat stimulation and a skin-absorbed analgesic.

Antacids

If you have baking soda in the kitchen, you have an antacid in the house, and it may be used as such if your need for it is *only* occasional and you are not on a low-salt diet for medical reasons (baking soda is high in sodium). If your need for an antacid is frequent, you ought to see your doctor about it. Meanwhile, if you buy a fizzy product, choose one that does not contain aspirin as one of its ingredients, lest you irritate your stomach even more.

Products containing calcium carbonate are known to have a rebound effect; they stimulate your stomach to produce more acid, even though they are neutralizing the acid you already have.

Cold Remedies

Although everyone says there is no cure for the common cold, Americans spend more money on cold relievers than on any other over-the-counter medicine.

Chicken soup, plain aspirin, and lots of fluids do a very creditable job of alleviating the common cold. Vitamin C or ascorbic acid is helpful, too, according to some doctors; other doctors disagree. While they are arguing the case, you might want to try vitamin C, which won't hurt you any, and see if it gives you relief. The usual dose is four 250 mg tablets per day. Some experts recommend that you take it two hours before or after you take your aspirin, because aspirin tends to wash vitamin C right out of your body by increasing urination.

You can take a product with antihistamine to relieve a runny nose, but you should keep in mind that it will increase mucus in the lungs. It will also make you sleepy.

Decongestants, as the name suggests, relieve congested nasal passages. They should not be used by persons with high blood pressure, heart disease, and a number of other ailments, so, as with all non-prescription drugs, read the labels carefully before you buy. Decongestants can have a rebound effect if you take too much; in other words, instead of clearing up those nasal passages, the "remedy" can suddenly cause them to swell if your system has had too much of the drug. This creates a vicious circle that can be avoided by minimum use of decongestants.

Neither decongestants nor antihistamines are strictly necessary additions to your medical supplies. If you do decide to stock them, the least complicated medication is the best, rather than a cold remedy containing aspirin and other ingredients. That way, you can control the amount of aspirin, decongestant, and antihistamine you are going to take, since at times you may want one without the other. For example, if someone in the house has a bout of hayfever, plain antihistamine will work to relieve that disorder, too, whereas a dose of aspirin may not be necessary.

Again, time-controlled antihistamine designed to last all night may not work exactly that way in your unique body. Absorption rates differ.

Nighttime cold remedies generally have an added percentage of alcohol (up to 25 percent). There is no particular advantage to taking alcohol with other medications; in fact, there is much evidence against the advisability of that practice.

Moist air in the sickroom can be helpful to the cold or flu sufferer. You can use a vaporizer or a plain tea kettle on a hot plate to accomplish this (the tea kettle must be watched, of course). Recent medical practice favors cold vapors over hot. Some people use a medication with the vaporizer, usually containing menthol or camphor. This is not necessary, but if you decide to mentholate the sickroom, it's better to use medication with a vaporizer than to use the aerosol sprays which are supposed to do the same thing. Those nasty propellents in the aerosol should not be breathed in directly.

[157]
*Assembling
Medical
Supplies—
Without Going
Broke*

Gargle

Plain warm salted water makes an effective gargle or mouthwash.

Diarrhea Remedies

Diarrhea accompanied by vomiting in infants and very young children is extremely dangerous, because fluids are being lost without being replaced, and small children dehydrate quickly. When this occurs, a doctor should be seen *that very day*.

Ordinary diarrhea not accompanied by vomiting in adults requires some treatment, so it is wise to have a remedy on hand and to take it with you when you travel. Kaopectate is a good one and available without prescription. Paregoric is good, too, but in most states you need a prescription to buy it. The victim of diarrhea also needs rest, fluids, and salt. Diarrhea with vomiting can be a symptom of food poisoning, and a doctor should be consulted.

Kaopectate can be used to control a pet's diarrhea, too. Consult your vet on proper dosage for your pet's size.

After Vomiting

Cola or ginger ale gone flat can be taken in little sips, or orange juice diluted with water. A sprinkle of salt is a good addition.

Constipation Remedies

Although diarrhea requires treatment, constipation may not, so it's really unnecessary to keep a remedy on hand. Many foods will supply a natural remedy for constipation. Outstanding among these are bran cereals, rhubarb (contained in some over-the-counter remedies), and dried fruits.

Many medical experts recommend that laxatives should not be taken at all. Mineral oil especially interferes with the body's absorption of nutrients and should not be taken plain to relieve constipation. In cases where stomach pain accompanies constipation, a laxative should *never* be taken. The pain might be caused by a swollen appendix, and a laxative could cause it to rupture.

Since milk of magnesia could be required as an antidote to some kinds of poisoning, if you're going to keep any laxative in the medicine cabinet, this one could serve a double purpose.

A number of drugs can cause constipation, among them sedatives and antacids. If you are taking either of these when constipation occurs, you might try simply stopping the use of the antacid or sedative. Constipation can be caused by certain diseases, too, so if it persists, medical attention should be sought.

Disinfectant

A disinfectant is a necessary part of your medical supplies. Plain alcohol is the best one for cleaning the skin around a wound, but since it stings an open cut, it is well to have a mild antiseptic cream to use on wounds that need it. Small clean cuts that bleed freely do not necessarily require any antiseptic other than soap and water, although medical opinions differ on that point. It is agreed, however, that a dirty cut, the kind of thing frequently seen on a child's knee, should be thoroughly but gently cleaned to remove the dirt.

Another point of general agreement is that soaking in hot soapy water is an effective treatment for an infected scratch or scrape. A doctor should be consulted when infection is present.

If you opt for the mild antiseptic cream, keep alcohol in your supplies anyway. It has dozens of sickroom uses, including sterilizing thermometers (rinse them in cool water afterward) and giving nice alcohol backrubs.

Bandages and Related Equipment

An adequate supply of bandaging equipment would include large and small sterile gauze pads and 1-inch adhesive tape, along with assorted adhesive bandage strips of various sizes. You also need small cotton bandages, a scissors, tweezers, large and small safety pins, sterile cotton, and something to make a sling, if necessary. Any triangular piece of material can serve as a sling, even a large scarf, or a square piece of sheeting folded into a triangle.

If a sudden need for sterile bandages exceeds your supply, you can make more of them by ironing laundered cloths (handkerchiefs, for instance) with a hot steam iron. Touch only the corners when applying the bandage to the wound.

Sterile bandages can be made in advance by placing the bandage material between two pieces of cloth and ironing thoroughly. Then keep the two pieces of material in place when storing, and they will protect the bandaging. Or boil laundered cloths for 15 minutes and dry them without touching them.

To keep a bandage in place, a nylon stocking can be used effectively over the dressing and sterile bandage. Nylon is a remarkably tough material.

Thermometers

It is useful to have both an oral and a rectal thermometer in your medicine cabinet if you have a very young child. Sterilize them after every use by dipping them in alcohol and then rinsing off the alcohol in cool water (never use hot water).

Poison Antidotes

In case of poisoning, expert advice must be sought immediately, and the recommended antidote should be in the medicine cabinet so that it can be quickly administered. Therefore, the following frequently prescribed antidotes should be among your medical supplies: syrup of ipecac, which is recommended when vomiting should be induced; activated charcoal, which is used to absorb any poison not removed by vomiting; epsom salts, milk of magnesia, baking soda, strong coffee, and vinegar are various other antidotes used for particular poisons. A full complement of poison antidotes should be a part of every home medical supply. For more on poison antidotes, see page 140.

Many cities and towns have established poison control centers. If your community has one, that is the best place to contact at once if you have an emergency.

[159]
*Assembling
Medical
Supplies—
Without Going
Broke*

Burn Remedies

Since the treatment of choice for burns these days is icewater, 41° to 55°F (5°–12°C), used until the burn is no longer painful, there is no need to stock any burn remedy.

For sunburn, too, no special remedy is needed. Some doctors recommend 2 tablespoons alcohol in 8 ounces of water for sunburn. Cold tea is an old-fashioned sunburn remedy that we find very effective.

Remedies for Bites, Stings, Poison Ivy, and Itches

If your family takes a lot of nature walks or goes backpacking, anything can happen, from a surfeit of mosquito bites to pitching a tent in a poison ivy patch. You may want to keep a soothing lotion among your medical supplies for the relief of these ills. Calamine lotion, although it has been around for a generation or two, is still recommened by many doctors. Calamine lotion can be used to soothe eczema, too.

Actually, though, recent tests have shown that plain hot water, between 120° and 130°F (50°–55°C), is a more effective remedy against itching than numerous over-the-counter preparations evaluated in the same tests. The hot water treatment can be given in the form of hot compresses.

A bath preparation can give relief from itching, also. Oatmeal is an excellent one (see page 116), and cornstarch is another effective remedy. The cornstarch bath is prepared by dissolving 1 cup cornstarch in a quart of cold water, then adding that mixture to your regular bath.

For bee stings or jellyfish stings, meat tenderizer which contains papain, a product of papaya, acts against the toxin. Other remedies are plain ammonia or a paste of baking soda and water for bee stings, and either vinegar or lemon juice for wasp stings (wasp toxin is an alkaloid).

Remedy for Plantar Warts

Speaking of hot water, another recent study showed that plantar warts on the sole of the foot can be treated with a foot bath of hot water, 120°F (50°C), and the warts will usually disappear within two weeks. Apparently hot water slows down the growth of the virus that is responsible for plantar warts.

Motion Sickness Remedy

If a member of the family is afflicted by motion sickness, you may want to keep a remedy such as Dramamine on hand. It can be used for pets, too (consult your vet as to proper dosage for your pet's size). Dramamine should not be taken at the same time as antibiotics. In case of "morning-sickness," neither Dramamine nor any other drug should be taken (see page 139 for some remedies for nausea). Dramamine makes the user sleepy.

Powder

A good absorbent powder for almost every purpose, from powdering your toes to powdering the baby, is ordinary cornstarch. It is more absorbent than talc, and, of course, starch is soothing to the skin in case of prickly heat or chafing. Cornstarch, unlike some other powders on the market—notably zinc stearate—is not toxic when inhaled. Its only drawback is that it cakes more easily than talc, so apply it lightly and evenly to avoid this.

Diaper Rash Remedy

In a full-blown case of diaper rash, more than powder is needed. If you can leave the baby bare-bottomed, this will clear up the problem at its source—an extra diaper can be folded and placed under baby's bottom to catch urine (admittedly, this is easier with girls than with boys). When diapers must be worn, a soothing antiseptic lotion or cream is needed. Look for a cream containing zinc oxide or hexachlorophene. The fewer antiseptic ingredients the better, since any of them can inspire a sensitivity. If that should happen, a product with several antiseptics will make it difficult to identify the culprit allergen.

Vitamins A and D (cod liver oil) are sometimes included in diaper rash ointments. To protect baby's skin before a rash happens, you can add a little cod liver oil to plain baby oil.

Athlete's Foot Remedy

When cracks between the toes, itching, and burning develop, treatment with foot powder is not sufficient. Look for a fungicide such as hexachlorophene.

Nerve Calmer

Usually advertised as a product for women, these combination pills are really a waste of money. They are just a combination of drugs you probably already have on hand: a buffered aspirin or aspirin substitute, antihistamine, and caffeine. The antihistamine calms you and the caffeine keeps you from falling asleep (maybe).

As a substitute a warm bath is a nerve calmer, too (not a hot shower, as both the hot water and the spray are energizers). A nice cup of tea will perk up the spirits. Add aspirin only if you really have a pain somewhere.

Vitamins and Minerals

Although opinion about their usefulness is mixed, we think it wise to have vitamin pills on hand, since there is quite a bit of empirical evidence on their behalf. For instance, there is much evidence that vitamin B complex fights mental stress. In the long run, taking a little extra vitamin B complex when life is trying is better for you than taking those nerve calmers sold over-the-counter whose calming ingredient is antihistamine, definitely a short-lived relief.

And, as we have mentioned before, we use vitamin C at the first sign of a sniffle. Vitamin C is helpful against any physical stress, and it is used up whenever there is a stress demand on the body. Vitamin C is also good for building up the gums if they have a tendency to bleed easily, or if you are prone to gum infections. (If gums bleed frequently, see your dentist.)

Recent studies have shown that vitamin E can be effective against menopausal symptoms and circulatory problems.

Improvised Sickroom Equipment

Three pillows, positioned like a pyramid, make a comfortable back rest for a bed-ridden patient. Sometimes it helps to have a small box braced between his feet and the foot of the bed to keep him from constantly slipping down.

If it is necessary to improvise a hospital bed at your house (which is a high bed that spares the nurse's back for easy patient care), choose a single bed because that will be easier to reach from all sides. Add an extra mattress to raise the bed to the desired height.

A crib-like arrangement can be improvised by putting two or three straight backed chairs on each side of the bed and roping them together to make a frame.

For a bed table, you can use an adjustable ironing board placed across the patient's legs and lowered to the desired height. Or a heavy cardboard box can be used by cutting out a tunnel for the patient's legs at the open end. If desired, hand holds can be cut in the sides, and it can even be covered with contact paper for an attractive washable surface.

Sources of Supplies

If some of the ingredients seem strange to you, don't be discouraged. All of the items used in this book are easily obtained from the sources listed below. Don't feel shy about asking for an ingredient. Whiting, for instance, may be unfamiliar to you, but to the clerk in a hardware store it's an everyday word.

You may not have a cosmetic supply house, a candle shop, or an herbalist in your neighborhood, but the mail order houses listed at the end of this appendix carry the things you'll need, and they'll be happy to fill your orders. Most mail order firms also provide catalogs upon request.

Acetone	Hardware store or paint store
Alcohol, denatured	Pharmacy
Alcohol, ethyl (vodka)	Liquor store
Alcohol, isopropyl	Pharmacy
Almond oil	Hardware store
Aloe gel	Health food store or pharmacy
Alum	Pharmacy
Ammonium chloride	Pharmacy
Amyl acetate	Pharmacy
Aniseed tea	Health food store or herbal supply house
Arrowroot	Supermarket
Ascorbic acid	Health food store
Balm	Herbal supply house
Banana oil	Pharmacy
Beeswax	Hobby center or candle supply shop
Benzene	Paint store or chemical supply house
Benzoin	Pharmacy
Bergamot, leaves	Herbal supply house
Bergamot, oil of	Pharmacy or herbal supply house
Bicarbonate of soda	Supermarket
Boric acid powder	Pharmacy
Borax	Hardware store or supermarket
Brewer's yeast	Health food store
Calamus, powdered	Perfume and cosmetic supply house
Camphor	Pharmacy
Carageenan	Health food store
Cardamom seed	Supermarket
Carnauba wax	Hobby center
Cassie extract	Perfume or cosmetic supply house
Castor oil	Pharmacy
Caustic soda (lye flakes)	Supermarket
Chamomile flowers	Herbal supply house
Charcoal, activated	Pharmacy
Charcoal, powdered	Pharmacy
Cinnamon, oil of	Pharmacy
Citral of geranial	Perfume or cosmetic supply house
Citronella, oil of	Pharmacy
Cleaning solvent	Hardware store
Cloves, powdered	Supermarket

Cocoa butter	Pharmacy
Cocoa powder	Supermarket
Color buds & liquid color	Hobby shop or candle supply shop
Color remover	Supermarket or hardware store
Copper sulfate	Pharmacy
Cosmetic color	Perfume and cosmetic supply house
Cream of tartar	Supermarket
Crystals for candles	Hobby shop or candle supply shop
Curry powder	Supermarket
Dichlorobenzene	Dye supply house or hardware store
Eucalyptus, oil of	Pharmacy
Fennel hair	Herbal supply house or supermarket
Fennel seeds	Supermarket
Flake salt	Supermarket or health food store
Formaldehyde (formalin)	Feed and grain store or chemical supply house
Fuller's earth	Ceramic supply store or hobby shop
Ginger root	Supermarket or herbal supply house
Glycerin	Pharmacy
Hydrated lime	Feed and grain store or pharmacy
Hydrochloric acid tablets	Pharmacy
Hydrogen peroxide	Pharmacy
Iodine	Pharmacy
Lanolin	Pharmacy
Lavender flowers	Perfume and cosmetic supply house
Lavender oil	Perfume and cosmetic supply house
Lemon, oil of	Pharmacy or perfume and cosmetic supply house
Licorice root	Herbal supply house
Lime, oil of	Pharmacy or perfume and cosmetic supply house
Linden blossoms	Herbal supply house
Linseed oil	Hardware store
Liquid Smoke	Supermarket
Logwood extract, powdered	Paint store or hardware store
Magnesium oxide	Feed and grain store or perfume and cosmetic supply house
Menthol	Pharmacy
Milk, powder or crystals	Supermarket
Mineral oil	Pharmacy
Mint leaves	Homegrown or herbal supply house
Napthalene flakes	Pharmacy or hardware store
Neat's-foot oil	Hardware store or dime store
Neroli, oil of	Pharmacy or perfume and cosmetic supply house
Orange leaves, dried	Perfume and cosmetic supply house
Orange water	Perfume and cosmetic supply house
Orris, extract	Perfume and cosmetic supply house
Orrisroot powder	Perfume and cosmetic supply house
Papaya	Health food store
Paraffin	Hobby shop or supermarket
Paraffin oil	Pharmacy or hardware store
Patchouly leaves	Perfume and cosmetic supply house
Patchouly, oil of	Pharmacy or perfume and cosmetic supply house
Pennyroyal	Herbal supply house
Peppermint, oil of	Pharmacy
Peppermint tea	Supermarket or health food store
Pepsin powder	Pharmacy
Petroleum jelly	Pharmacy or supermarket
Plaster of Paris	Hardware store
Precipitated chalk	Pharmacy
Pumice powder	Hardware store
Rice powder	Pharmacy or cosmetic supply house

Rose hips	Health food store
Rose, oil of	Pharmacy or perfume and cosmetic supply house
Rosemary, dried	Supermarket
Rose water	Pharmacy or perfume and cosmetic supply house
Rosin	Hardware store or music store
Rottenstone powder	Hardware store
Safflower oil	Supermarket or health food store
Sal soda	Supermarket or chemical supply house
Sandalwood, extract	Perfume and cosmetic supply house
Sandalwood, ground	Perfume and cosmetic supply house
Sandalwood, oil of	Perfume and cosmetic supply house
Scents	Hobby shop, candle supply store, or perfume supply house
Sesame seed oil	Supermarket or health food store
Sodium perborate	Pharmacy
Sodium sesquicarbonate	Pharmacy or chemical supply house
Sodium silicate	Pharmacy
Sodium thiosulfate	Photographic supply store
Stearin	Hobby shop or candle supply shop
Steel wool 0000	Hardware store
Strawberry, oil of	Perfume and cosmetic supply house
Sulfur, powdered	Pharmacy or hardware store
Tallow	Supermarket meat section
Tannic acid	Pharmacy or chemical supply house
Tansy	Homegrown or herbal supply house
Tragacanth, powdered	Pharmacy or chemical supply house
Trisodium phosphate	Hardware store
Turmeric	Supermarket
Turpentine	Hardware store
Verbana, extract of	Perfume and cosmetic supply house
Violet extract	Perfume and cosmetic supply house
Violet leaves, dried	Perfume and cosmetic supply house
Walnut leaves, dried	Homegrown or perfume and cosmetic supply house
Wheat, cracked	Supermarket or health food store
Wheat germ oil	Supermarket or health food store
Whey	Dairy or from homemade yogurt or cheese
Whiting (powdered chalk)	Hardware store
Wick	Hobby shop or candle supply shop
Wintergreen, oil of	Pharmacy
Witch hazel	Pharmacy
Yeast, dry	Supermarket

For perfume, cosmetic, or herbal needs:
Caprilands Herb Farms
Silver Street
North Coventry, Connecticut 06238

Caswell-Massey Company, Ltd.
320 West 13th Street
New York, New York 10014

For candlemaking supplies:
General Supplies Company
P.O. Box 338
Fallbrook, California 92028

The Candle Shop
Goode, Virginia 24556

Metric Conversion Table

Ounces	Grams	Pounds	Kilograms
$1/2$	14	$1/2$	.2
1	28	1	.4
2	57	2	.9
3	85	3	1.4
4	113	4	1.8
5	142	5	2.3
10	284	10	4.5

Cups	Milliliters	Pints	Milliliters
$1/4$	59	$1/2$	237
$1/3$	79	1	475
$1/2$	118	2	950
$2/3$	158		
$3/4$	177		
1	237		
2	475		

Quarts	Liters	Gallons	Liters
1	.95	1	3.8
2	1.90	2	7.6
3	2.85	3	11.4
4	3.80	4	15.0

Teaspoons	Milliliters	Tablespoons	Milliliters
$1/4$	1.25	1	15
$1/2$	2.50	2	30
$3/4$	3.75	3	45
1	5.00	4	60
2	10.00	5	75

Inches	Centimeters
$1/2$	1.3
1	2.5
2	5.0
3	7.5
4	10.0
5	12.5
6	15.0
10	25.4

Index

The index, like the text, is divided into four sections:
Household Products, Foods, Cosmetics, and Home Remedies.

HOUSEHOLD PRODUCTS

Ammonia, warning about mixing with
    chlorine bleach, 4

Bathroom cleaners, 15–17
    disinfectant, 16
    floor, 16
    grout, 16
    plastic accessories, 17
    tile, 16
Beeswax, 5, 45, 59
Book(s)
    binding repair, 59
    dusting and care, 23
    mildewed, 24
    paste, 59
Bricks, cleaning, 21

Candlemaking, 44–52
    beeswax, 45
    container candles, 51
    crystals, 46
    dyes, 46–47
    glazing, 50–51
    hurricane candles, 51–52
    molds, 45–46, 47, 49, 50
    paraffin, 44
    precautions, 40, 41, 44
    scents, 47
    stearin, 46
    supplies, 44–48
    tools, 52
    utensils, 47–48
    wicks, 45
Carpet cleaning, 21
Cement, 59. *See also* Glues and pastes
Chinaware repair, cement, 59
Chlorine bleach, warning about mixing with
    ammonia, 4
Citronella candles, bug repellant, 56–57
Cleaning formulas
    andirons, 22
    bathroom, 15–17
    books, 23, 24
    bricks, 21
    carpets, 21
    drains, 9
    fireplaces, 21–22
    floors, 19–20
    flowerpots, 23
    furniture, 4–7
    glass, 20
    jewelry, 14–15
    kitchen, 9–12, 43
    laundry, 35–38
    leather and suede, 22
    marble, 22, 23
    painted surfaces, 19
    plastic, 17, 23
    slate, 22
    spots and stains, 24–35
    stone, 21
    tile, 16
    upholstery, 20–21
    wallpaper, 19
    walls, 18–19
    woodwork, 19
Combs, cleaning, 17

Deodorizers, deodorants, and disinfectants,
    16–18, 21
    for hands, 17
    household, 17–18
    laundry, 36
    pet urine, 21
Dyes
    in candlemaking, 46
    stain removal, 28–29

Fireplace cleaning, 21–22
Flame retardants, for clothes, 36–37
Floor cleaners, 19–20. *See also* Wax removal
    concrete, 24
    mildewed, 24
Floor polishing, 19
Food stains, 29, 31, 32, 34, 35. *See also* Spot
    and stain removal
Food washing, 11, 56
Furniture cleaning and care, 4–7
    plastic (outdoor), 23

COSMETICS

Plantar warts remedy, 160. *See also* Athlete's foot
Poison antidotes, 159
Poisoning
  diarrhea as symptom of, 157
  emergency action, 140, 159
Poison ivy, 140, 159
Powder. *See also* **Cosmetics**—Powders
  for athlete's foot, 160
  for chafing and prickly heat, 160
  cornstarch, 160
Prickly heat, 138–139

Remedies. *See also* Medical supplies
  for athlete's foot, 160
  bites and stings, 159
  burns, 159
  chafing and prickly heat, 160
  colds, 158
  constipation, 158
  diaper rash, 160
  diarrhea, 157
  itching, 139. *See also* Itching
  motion sickness, 160
  nervousness, 160
  pain relievers, 155–156
  plantar warts, 160
  poison antidotes, 159
  poison ivy, 140, 159
  stomach acid, 139, 156

toothache, 144
after vomiting, 157

Sensitivity (of skin). *See* Allergies
Shock, 140
Sickroom equipment, 161
Sore throat, 141
Sprains, 141
Sties, 141
Stings (insects), 135, 159
Stress, 161
Sunburn, 159

Tannin (in tea), 153
Tea. *See* Medicinal foods
Thermometers, 159
Tisanes (herbal teas). *See* Plant medicine and herbal teas
Tooth ache, 141

Vitamin C, 161
  for bruises, 136
  for colds, 137, 156, 161
  in foods, 147, 150, 152
  for hay fever, 137
Vitamins and minerals, for treatment of symptoms, 161
Vomiting, 157

Wine. *See* Medicinal foods